The Writing of Co
Adrift in Soho

Including Charles Russell's
The Other Side of Town

Edited by Colin Stanley

[Colin Wilson Studies #26]

Paupers' Press

Published by:
Paupers' Press,
37 Quayside Close,
Turney's Quay,
Nottingham NG2 3BP
England.

Printed and bound in the UK by PublishPoint
from KnowledgePoint Limited, Reading.
I.S.B.N. 9780956866370 (Paperback)
I.S.S.N. 0959-180-X (Colin Wilson Studies #26)

Every effort has been made to trace living relatives of Sidney R. Campion
and Charles Russell. If anyone has any information please contact us at the
e-mail address below:

For our complete catalogue of books, write to the above address or e-mail
us at: **books@pauperspress.com**

Contents

The Writing of *Adrift in Soho*

Colin Stanley

Adrift in Soho was Colin Wilson's second published novel. It appeared on September 4, 1961 in the trademark yellow Victor Gollancz dust-jacket and was published six weeks later by Houghton Mifflin in the US. Released one year after *Ritual in the Dark*, it is a semi-autobiographical coming-of-age story, set in the 1950s, about a young man from the provinces searching for freedom in London. In his autobiography, *Dreaming to Some Purpose* (2004), Wilson explained that the novel had, in fact, started out as a collaboration between himself and an old Soho friend called Charles Belchier, otherwise known as Charles Russell, a Bohemian actor who appeared uncredited as the bandleader on the *Titanic* in the film *A Night to Remember* (1958):

> We had not been close friends in my Soho days, for Charles, like so many actors, was uninterested in ideas, so we had little in common. But after *The Outsider* came out, he contacted me, and came to stay with us on several occasions. And he asked my help finding a publisher for an unfinished autobiographical book called *The Other Side of Town*. As soon as I read it I saw that it was unpublishable in its present form—it was too short, and had no development. But the fragment fascinated me....For about a week I tried to rewrite it as a novel, then suddenly realised that I could not write the book from behind Charles's eyes, so to speak; I had to put myself into it. So it turned into a story about a provincial youth who, like myself, has worked as a navvy in an attempt to

1

avoid office work, and who goes to London in search of a more interesting life. (Wilson, 2004, p.223)

In his Introduction to his later novel *The Killer*, Wilson described Russell as a "charming and intelligent man…" but:

> [he] was unsuccessful in his chosen profession—as an actor….His first response to his lack of success was to create a theory to the effect that modern society is an intolerable strait-jacket for 'free-spirits' and that an amoral 'bohemian' existence was the only answer. As the problem became more acute he became a racialist who felt that England had no place for his talents…
> (Wilson 1970, p. 10)

In the event, Russell was paid £100 for his manuscript and it was agreed that he should receive a small percentage of the royalties. When interviewed by *The Sunday Express* on September 10, 1961 he said:

> "I do not mind. Originally I sent my book to Colin for him to do a preface. I was then going to sell it. But he said he would like to re-write it and I agreed. Money would be useful but I am a Bohemian and want freedom more than anything else".

Soon after the book was published, Wilson and Russell appeared on a Westward Television arts programme in which they appeared to argue over authorship and even staged a mock fight in front of the cameras. This had apparently been arranged between them beforehand in the hope of drumming-up some publicity for the novel and backfired somewhat because it was totally overlooked and not reported in any newspapers the following day.

The character that Wilson introduced was Harry Preston and a short Prologue describes his working life in the East Midlands (almost certainly based on Wilson's home town of Leicester) after being dismissed from the RAF (as, indeed, Wilson himself had been) and before making the decision to seek his fortune in the Capital. After this Prologue, the book is divided into two parts. In Part One, Harry arrives at St Pancras station and seeks accommodation at the Youth Hostel in Great Ormond Street. He then takes a tube ride from Russell Square to Leicester Square, walks up Charing Cross Road and has a cheap meal in a café on Tottenham Court Road. Retracing his steps, he has a drink in a pub on the corner of Old Compton Street, reflecting gloomily on the impersonal nature of the metropolis:

> The whole city was a part of the great unconscious conspiracy of matter to make you feel non-existent...It is a monument to your unimportance, a perpetual gesture of disrespect from the universe to people who lack a sense of their own necessity. (p. 22)

The next day he sets about finding lodgings. Using a copy of the *London Weekly Advertiser*, he finds an attic room in Courtfield Gardens, Earl's Court, for two pounds fifteen shillings a week and decides, in order to save money, to spend much of his time in Kensington Public Library.

Back in the pub, however, he meets James Compton Street—an out-of-work actor—who takes him under his wing and escorts him into Soho for a meal (for which Harry, of course, pays). The rich character of James is based upon Charles Belchier himself who is, in fact, *called* Charles in the US

3

editions. For fear that some acquaintance should claim to be identified in the novel, Gollancz's legal advisers suggested that the name be completely changed to James Gerrard Street because Belchier often signed himself as 'Compton Street'. A compromise was eventually arrived at.

Very much a charmer, James picks-up a young girl and persuades Harry to let them use his room for the night. Inevitably the landlady finds out and Harry is given his marching orders. His subsequent low opinion of landladies parallels Wilson's own after *his* move to London in June 1951:

> Why did such people exist? Why did she want to browbeat fellow human beings? It would be a very satisfying world in which her kind could be struck dead by the loathing they aroused...(p. 30)

Back in Soho, James introduces him to a number of colourful characters including the 'King of the Bohemians' himself: Ironfoot Jack. Jack, otherwise known as 'Professor' J. R. Neave, was a real character who frequented Soho at that time. His right leg was shorter than his left and to overcome this he wore a surgical boot with an iron extension below the sole. His favourite haunt was the French coffee bar on Old Compton Street where he would often talk to friends and students from the nearby St Martin's Art School on literature, art, philosophy, music and the occult. He carried a blue cloth bag around with him containing second-hand books, newspaper cuttings, notebooks and the typed manuscript of his 'Memoirs'. This manuscript was left by Neave to Wilson in the late 1950s (just before he died sometime in 1959) in the hope that he might find a publisher for it. Despite several attempts, however, he was unsuccessful and I recently came across the manuscript when sorting Wilson's papers prior to them being deposited in his archive at the University of Nottingham. I am now in the process of editing it for publication, sometime in 2017.

It would appear that the inspiration for the hilarious fish-and-chip meal at Osky's, recounted in *Adrift...*, came from Ironfoot Jack who recalls, in his 'Memoirs', being told about such an establishment although he was not able to verify the story personally.

James proposes to Harry that they form a "league for mutual support" in which they take it in turns to support each other for two weeks, using James's know-how to live as cheaply as they can without working. He then proceeds to introduce Harry to the "Compton Street breakfast tour" which involves sleeping on the midnight train from Waterloo to Staines, hitch-hiking back to London and freshening-up in the washrooms of the British Museum. Wilson, when famously sleeping rough on Hampstead Heath to save money, in the mid-1950s, made use of these very facilities himself before spending the rest of the day in the Reading Room working on *Ritual In the Dark* and, what was eventually his first published book: *The Outsider*.

This way of life soon palls, however, and Harry comes to regret his bargain, longing for solitude and a room of his own where he can read, write and think. It is this attitude that turns the novel into "a deliberate counterblast against all the 'Beat Generation' philosophy and 'Angry Young Man' stuff", as Wilson wrote in a letter to his publisher. Those critics who described *Adrift...* as an English 'beat' novel, failed to appreciate that Wilson was not glorifying this way of life, as Russell's manuscript no doubt had; quite the reverse. Wilson himself had by then already 'escaped' from all that and from the round of London literary parties, functions etc, with which he had become embroiled, after the success of *The Outsider* in 1956, and moved

5

away to Cornwall in order to pursue his life's work in peace and quiet.

Harry meets a young girl from New Zealand, Doreen, and together they move into a room in a house in Notting Hill. This was based on Wilson's own lodgings, during the mid-1950s, at 24 Chepstow Villas but again Gollancz's legal advisers stepped-in suggesting he make the location a little vaguer: it is described in the novel as the "Ladbroke Road house". In 'My Night with the Beatniks,' an article written for the *Sunday Dispatch* on January 15, 1961, Wilson describes a night spent at a Beat commune in London researching *Adrift*.... Unconvinced of the soundness of Beat philosophy, he wrote: "I give the whole craze another three years." The article itself caused some concern and was discussed in the House of Lords. A piece in *The Times* on February 8, 1961 reported that Lord Amulree thought the references to marijuana and Preludin in the article might be deemed an incitement to commit an offence. Earl Bathurst, Lord in Waiting, replied that the article had been referred to the Director of Public Prosecutions who, fortunately for Wilson, felt there was insufficient grounds for prosecution. It was probably here that Wilson drew his inspiration for the scene at the end of Part One where Harry smokes marijuana and finds "the kind of muzzy happiness it created was the enemy of incisive thought or feeling" (p. 155). Despite the 'swinging sixties', Wilson maintained this stance, against the use of drugs to induce higher states of consciousness, preferring more intellectually-based methods.

It is at this stage that *Adrift*... moves on from Russell's memoir, away from Soho and into the much shorter Part Two of the novel. Wilson wrote in *Dreaming to Some Purpose*: "I soon used up all Charles's plot, and decided to extend it with bits of my play *The Metal Flower Blossom*." (Wilson, 2004, p. 224)

The Writing of *Adrift in Soho*

This had been written by Wilson, in the early 1950s, for a group of teenagers, including the budding novelist Laura Del Rivo, who spent their evenings around Soho. When the group split up, and Wilson went off to Paris, the play remained unperformed and had to wait until December 11, 1960 for its premiere at the Palace Theatre, Westcliff-on-Sea—a one-off performance in front of an audience of 500. It did not appear in print as a play until 2008 when an anthology entitled *'The Death of God' and other plays* was published by Paupers' Press.

The central character is a Bohemian artist by the name of Ricky Prelati and it concerns him and the weird assortment of characters that drift in and out of his studio:

> Because it was written for a group of friends, I wrote without the kind of inhibitions that might have bothered me if I was writing a "real play". I tossed in a Hindu yogi, a devil worshipper...and a mad ballet choreographer....I also threw in a naked model, a lady evangelist and a homosexual. (These were the days when homosexuality was illegal, and it was still regarded as vaguely scandalous). (Wilson, 2008, p. 12)

It was this content, no doubt, that caused Lady Astor to ban its proposed production at Plymouth Arts Centre in 1957.

Like James, Ricky Prelati seeks freedom but whereas James drifts, Prelati creates. This need to create appeals to Harry and he goes off to the British Museum with the intention of making notes for a volume on the nature of freedom. The novel ends when Prelati's work is discovered and, much to his disgust, he achieves fame overnight in the manner in which Wilson himself had achieved it in 1956, after the publication of *The Outsider*. Victor Gollancz was happy with the indeterminate

The Writing of *Adrift in Soho*

ending, writing to Wilson that "it produces an effect like a Viennese *perpetuum mobile...*" Sidney R. Campion, in his study of Wilson's early work, *The Sound Barrier* concluded:

> "...the indeterminate ending might be said to be prescribed by the subject. Even if [it] had continued for another fifty pages, there would have been no real ending....Harry Preston confront[s] a certain 'existential problem', a problem about the nature of freedom. [His] experiences in the course of the novel provide material for a solution...[it is] not the novelist's job to offer the solution to the reader." (Campion, 2011, p. 125-6)

Despite the impression, given in this essay, of a somewhat disjointed hodge-podge, the novel works remarkably well. The evocation of Soho, during that fascinating period in the 1950s, and the descriptions of some of its characters, bring a vibrancy to the narrative. Anthony Rhodes in the *Times Literary Supplement* (Sept. 8, 1961, p. 593) wrote "From the moment the story opens the reader is lost, spellbound..." and predicted: "This is a small book—and in Mr. Wilson's work it may well prove to be a minor one—but it is surely a signpost to a distinguished career as a novelist." Nicolas Tredell in his study *Novels to Some Purpose: the fiction of Colin Wilson* wrote:

> *Adrift in Soho*, for all its lightness, manages to be many things. A *Bildungsroman*; a picaresque tale; a documentary; a period piece; a fairy story; an investigation of freedom. After *Ritual in the Dark*, worked over many times, brooded-on obsessively by Wilson, it is a kind of release, a burst of light-heartedness. It also teaches a lesson relevant to Wilson's

8

The Writing of *Adrift in Soho*

future development as a novelist: that an apparently light-weight form could deal with serious themes. (Tredell, 2016, p. 123)

Sidney R. Campion described *Adrift...* as "Wilson's lightest work—from the point of view of size as well as content" and it *is* true that this is not the usual novel of ideas we expect from Wilson the philosopher-novelist. But there are moments when insights break through such as when Harry is "overwhelmed by a kind of brainstorm of insight" whilst walking down Tottenham Court Road, catching a glimpse of some illustrations of Egyptian statues through the window of a bookshop: "Something about their mathematical perfection excited me...made me tremble...." (p. 72). He recalls a similar "brainstorm", when he was sixteen, which had encouraged him to "devote some time to clarify my vision of 'life as it might be', and the attempt brought me a new sense of purpose and concentration" (p. 71). This is the theme that permeates all of Wilson's work whether writing about philosophy, psychology, criminology, music, literature or any of the many other subjects he set his mind to.

The novel was published in paperback by Pan Books in 1964 and translated into French and Spanish but, after the mid-1960s, remained out-of-print in the UK for 25 years becoming a much sought-after Wilson title; second-hand first editions changing hands for very high prices. Then in 1993 it was reprinted by Brainiac Books, with a cover illustration by Barbara Bennett, depicting a duffle-coated Wilson, sitting under Eros at Piccadilly Circus. In 2011 it was reprinted again by Five Leaves as part of their 'Beatniks, Bums and Bohemians' series anticipating the film, directed by Pablo Behrens, shot in Nottingham and London, that is (at May 2016) still in production by Burning Films: www.adriftinsoho.com

The Writing of *Adrift in Soho*

In his autobiography, *Dreaming to Some Purpose*, Wilson recounts the rather tragic conclusion to Charles Russell's life:

> In the summer of 1968, he wrote to me from some island in the Mediterranean, telling me that he had found the perfect way of life, beach-combing, dozing in the sun and smoking pot. Six months or so later, I received a press cutting from his girlfriend: it is from the *Daily Express* of 6 December 1968:
>
> > "A 43-year-old Englishman arrested for peddling dangerous drugs in West Germany committed suicide in his cell in Heilbronn today. He was named as Charles Belchier of no fixed address.
> >
> > He and two associates were arrested after they were found with hashish worth £1,500 on the black market."
>
> Apparently Charles had hanged himself. (Wilson, 2004, p. 224)

In the aforementioned Introduction to *The Killer* he concluded "I was sad to hear of his death; but I could honestly think of no way in which he could have adjusted himself to the reality of the world he lived in." (Wilson, 1970, p. 10)

Page numbers refer to the 2011 edition of *Adrift in Soho* (Nottingham: Five Leaves Publications)

Suggested reading:

Campion, Sidney R. (1962) *The World of Colin Wilson: a biographical study*. London: Frederick Muller Limited.

The Writing of *Adrift in Soho*

Campion, Sidney R. (2011) *The Sound Barrier: a study of the ideas of Colin Wilson*. Nottingham: Paupers' Press.

Farson, Daniel (1987) *Soho in the Fifties*. London: Michael Joseph.

Miles, Barry (2010) *London Calling: a countercultural history of London since 1945*. London: Atlantic Books.

Stanley, Colin (ed) (2011) *Around the Outsider: essays presented to Colin Wilson on the occasion of his 80th birthday*. Winchester: 0-Books.

Stanley, Colin (2016) *The Ultimate Colin Wilson Bibliography, 1956-2016*. Nottingham: Paupers' Press.

Tredell, Nicolas (2016) *Novels to Some Purpose: the fiction of Colin Wilson*. Nottingham: Paupers' Press.

Wilson, Colin (1956) *The Outsider*. London: Gollancz.

Wilson, Colin (1960) *Ritual in the Dark*. London: Gollancz. reprinted by Valancourt Books (with an Introduction by Colin Stanley), 2013.

Wilson, Colin (1970) *The Killer*. London: New English Library.

Wilson, Colin (2004) *Dreaming to Some Purpose*. London: Century.

Wilson, Colin (2008) *'The Death of God' and other plays*. Nottingham: Paupers' Press.

The Colin Wilson Collection is at the University of Nottingham, King's Meadow Campus, Lenton Lane, Nottingham NG7 2NR United Kingdom, and now includes many of the author's manuscripts

Unpublished Author's Note to *Adrift in Soho.*

Colin Wilson

About two years ago, an out-of-work actor named Charles Russell sent me the manuscript of his autobiography, *The Other Side of Town*. This came to interest me for reasons quite other than those that Charles expected. His book was a typical 'Beat Generation' document, describing a drifting and slightly criminal existence in Soho. It was full of real people and purports to expound Charles's philosophy of freedom—which is more-or-less identical with that of Jack Kerouac. It might be summarized in Rousseau's words: "Man is born free and is everywhere in chains".

All this fascinated me because this rejection of society is the poet's primary impulse, expressed by Wordsworth in the sonnet 'The world is too much with us'. And yet between this impulse to reject the sordid 'getting and spending' of the bourgeois, and the equally sordid, futile life that Charles described so naively, something has very plainly gone wrong. In rewriting his manuscript, I wanted to ask the question: "What went wrong?". In short, I wanted to produce a counterblast to the ideology of the 'Beat Generation', a kind of T. E. Hulme-like criticism of unlimited romanticism.

In my first attempt at rewriting I tried to simply expand Charles's original version. Here I ran into a great difficulty that baffled me for a year. Since Charles was the narrator of my novel, I had to make him do a lot of rather silly and immoral things; and yet those actions were incompatible with the kind of sensitivity I wanted to give *my* narrator. After a long time it came to me that I would have to put the material into the mouth of another narrator. This young man, who is more closely identified with me, came from a Midland town, and goes to London (at the end of Chapter One) 'in search of freedom'. There he meets Charles who offers to show him how to achieve freedom in Soho and who leads him through Soho as Virgil led Dante!

Here I met with another difficulty. I was thoroughly enjoying inventing incidents and characters in the picaresque manner; but even a picaresque novel must move towards a conclusion. My narrator soon feels that the kind of freedom Charles advocates is not freedom at all; but this is a purely negative conclusion. So, in the second part of the book, the narrator becomes closely acquainted with Ricky Prelati, the painter, whom he feels to be a man with a more classical notion of freedom—the self-discipline of the artist. Ricky is so preoccupied with his need to bring his art to perfection that he actually does his best to avoid recognition until he has learned to express himself with the clarity he imagines.

In a sense, then, Book One might be called 'Charles' and Book Two: 'Ricky'. Plainly, there is no ending to the book; but the shape of the book is determined by the narrator's consideration of the meaning of freedom in society.

I have said that Charles and Ironfoot Jack are the only two characters based on real people. This is literally true. I should add that the narrator is *not* me, and none of the things that happen to him have ever happened to me. I never knew Charles when I first came to London, and never went around Soho with him.

Although the present version of the book owes only its original conception to Charles, I have agreed to give him £100 in exchange for his agreement to allow me to use his material. I shall also make an agreement to allot to Charles some small proportion of the royalties in the event of the book being a best-seller (not a very likely one) or of film rights being sold. It is possible that a prefatory note might be advisable, explaining Charles's part in the book. He is very much a sleeping partner in the venture; David Bolt will get him to sign an agreement in exchange for the £100, selling me the 'autobiography' outright.

It is true, of course, that Charles is not a necessary part of the bargain. If the name of my character was changed from Charles to Robert, and his profession changed from actor to photographer or commercial artist, 'Charles' would become unrecognizable, and would, I think, have no right to claim that he plays any part in the novel at all. However, when the agreement is signed and the money paid over, I see no reason why Charles should not remain in the novel as Charles. He is only too happy to be identified with the central character; he naturally hopes that it might make his name known and open up opportunities in the theatre. I have taken great care not to condemn Charles openly in the book, and have said nothing about him that he has not already said in his 'autobiography'.

Finally, it should be added that 'Charles' is a fictional portrait, although based on the real Charles. He is less like the real Charles than Isherwood's Mr. Norris, for example, is like Gerald Hamilton.

Adrift in Soho

Sidney R. Campion

[Extracted from *The World of Colin Wilson* (London: Frederick Muller Limited, 1962]

In a television interview, Wilson dismissed his novel, *Adrift in Soho*, as a pot-boiler. This comment seemed to me to be misleading; although the book is Wilson's slightest work to date, it develops many of the ideas of *The Outsider*.

I was also aware that one of its central characters—'James Compton Street'—was a very real person, since I met him in a pub in Poppins Court, Fleet Street, lunching off bread and cheese and a glass of beer, when he told me that he was collaborating with Colin on a book.

Adrift in Soho appeared in late September 1961, and was, generally speaking, better received by the critics than any of Wilson's books since *The Outsider*. I suspected that this was because it was the least ambitious of his books and contained no general ideas; it could therefore be judged simply as a novel; and as a novel it is undoubtedly well written and very amusing. I wondered whether the author's attempt to dismiss it as a pot-boiler was only another effort to mislead the critics who might dislike it as a novel of ideas? This question drew forth the following letter from Colin:

Oct. 2nd, 1961.

"My Dear Sidney,
Thank you for your kind remarks about *Soho*. The *Sunday Express* story is accurate as far as it goes. The book was certainly

based on Charles Russell's manuscript, although not nearly as much as the *Express* piece suggests.

What actually happened was this: I met Charles in Soho in 1953, just after I had separated from my wife, Betty. He was known as the heart-throb of all the Soho girls. Even in those days he always described himself as an "out of work actor". I hardly knew him; in fact, I didn't really speak to him until after *The Outsider* was published.

One day he sent me the manuscript of a kind of autobiographical novel called *The Other Side of Town*. I get lots of manuscripts in my post, and usually send them straight back to their authors. However, I glanced at Charles's manuscript—it was only about 60 pages—and was very amused. The style was tight and witty—although it reminded me of Peter Cheyney. (Its opening sentence was: "Take your tongue out of my ear.") Charles described very openly how he bummed around Soho, and "conned" people for money. He also spent a lot of the book expounding his philosophy of freedom—that modern society is corrupt, and such people as he are honest enough to "opt out" and refuse to play the game.

I was very excited by this book—not because I thought it well written, but because I could remember feeling exactly like Charles when I first came to London. London is full of people like Charles; people who are too talented and mercurial to accept a routine job, and yet not talented enough to dictate their own terms to society and live off their talent. But even the most talented man can doubt himself, and wonder whether society will accept him at his own valuation. So all these people—all the would-be artists—are in the same boat. Supposing society will never acknowledge your right not to work at a routine job? Supposing that it will never pay you for "expressing yourself" on paper or canvas? You have two

Sidney R. Campion

alternatives—to capitulate and take a job, or to live like Charles, taking what you can get as your "right", since society refuses to give it.

Of course, there is the third line of action: to take a routine job, and work patiently at your books or paintings in your spare time, until recognition comes. But this may require more patience or strength than you possess. In that case, what do you do? According to Charles, you pit your cunning against society and pursue the "philosophy of freedom".

One objection had occurred to me. I had tried living "outside society" for years, and found it boring and demoralising. All the stories about "la Bohéme" are untrue. However, Charles's book excited me. Admittedly, it had no depth. But it posed the basic problem, the same problem posed by America's Beat generation: do we need a new "class" in our society, a class of "dharma bums"? Our society is too rigid; there is too big a gap between the unsuccessful would-be artist and the successful artist. Is it any wonder if any of the misfits become criminals?

I decided that I would re-write Charles's book. I would give its central character the kind of depth that he did not at present possess; he would become a "displaced metaphysician". Charles came down here to Cornwall to provide me with additional information and I began to work on the book in the winter of 1959. However, it was hopeless. The narrator was still Charles, but a Charles who no longer over-simplified the intellectual issues. But here a problem arose. I had to make Charles do various discreditable things, like swindling girls in the National Gallery, etc. But this was completely inconsistent with the kind of sensitivity and intelligence I had given him as a narrator. I was baffled and abandoned the book.

17

Sidney R. Campion

Then one day, looking through some of your letters—you must be our most prolific letter-writer—I read how you were once baffled when attempting a portrait bust of Eustacia Vye who so captivated you whenever you read *The Return of the Native*. You, too, abandoned the effort, but only temporarily. You hid the unfinished work for a few weeks, and when you brought it out into the full daylight and saw it afresh, your creative spirit found a new force and you quickly finished the bust. Reading that gave me a new impetus, and when I saw the story again the solution came to me. I decided to keep Charles as the central character, and to introduce a narrator, a young man who goes to Soho from a Midland town and who is also searching for the elusive "freedom". He meets Charles in Soho, and Charles offers to show him how to avoid working for a living.

Under this fresh stimulus I wrote the book in January 1960. I ran out of adventures—Charles's supply was very short—and so I used chunks of my play, *The Metal Flower Blossom* (remember Ricky Prelati?), and included a lot of anecdotes told to me by my neighbour, John Pennell. Then I sent the manuscript to my publisher before it was completed, and he liked it so much as it stood that there was no need to add more, and that explains why the book is not actually finished.

There was an amusing incident after publication. Following the *Express* story about Charles and myself, we were invited to appear on television together, and it was suggested that we should have a good row. We agreed, and I said I would try to defend myself if Charles wanted to accuse me of "stealing" his book. In the midst of his argument with me on the programme, he leapt suddenly to his feet with his back to the camera and pretended to give me a tremendous blow on the chin.

Sidney R. Campion

The interviewer had to separate us, and I had great difficulty in preventing myself from smiling. To my amazement and relief, the incident did not receive a single comment in the Press."

I rebuked Colin at the time, and I rebuke him now, for allowing himself to become involved in such an episode. He is now of a stature when his public image should evoke admiration and respect. It is not enough to say that he did it largely for the benefit of Charles Russell.

'My Night With the Beatniks'

Colin Wilson

[First published in *The Sunday Dispatch*, January 15, 1961.]

I always take a sleeping bag to London—you never know when you might need it.

Only a few weeks ago on one of my periodic trips to town I was looking for somewhere to stay. A girl with whom I was drinking in a Soho bar said: "Come on back to my place."

"Won't your landlady mind?" I asked.

She seemed vastly amused by this suggestion. Soon I was to find out why....

At one in the morning we drove to a narrow road between Chelsea and World's End. We climbed three flights of uncarpeted stairs and went into an enormous L-shaped room. From outside it sounded as if there was a party going on, but when we got inside I discovered that the music was being made by a long-haired Beatnik strumming a guitar. About ten people were lying around on cushions or on massive camp beds, and one of them was reading aloud from a bulky manuscript. It seemed to be a kind of poetry without metres.

The girl, who I will call Myra, told me he had just completed a long poem aiming at the overthrow of civilization and was reading it to flamenco music, which suited its mood. I sat down and listened for half an hour, then whispered,

"When does the party break up?"

"It doesn't," Myra said, "we all live here."

The next day I learned how a beat community was run. A dozen of them—eight men and four girls—had rented a whole floor of the house. The landlady lived in Kensington and didn't care what went on, so long as they didn't wreck the place. They never slept until four in the morning and they got up at midday. Then some of them went off to the Charing Cross Road to steal books; others to steal food from self-service stores. Most of the food was thrown into one huge cooking pot and boiled into a stew. I watched it being made—bacon, apples, raisins, cheese, tins of sardines and tins of soup—I ate a basinful myself. It was pretty horrible—mainly because someone had emptied a whole bottle of lemon juice in "to improve the flavour".

Music was played during all the meals—either the guitar or a gramophone. The favourite records were Charlie Parker (the god of the Beat Generation) and the Modern Jazz Quartet. Cheap Spanish wine was drunk in quantity.

No one had his own room—you slept anywhere you felt inclined. The girls, like everything else, were communal. Although they were all vaguely attached to particular men, there was no dog-in-the-manger spirit, and they shared out their affections impartially. There was always a casual influx of layabouts who needed somewhere to sleep, so the men usually outnumbered the women. Myra was particularly popular, and she solved the problem in her own way by spending the first part of the night with one man then moving on to another.

In spite of the complete lack of discipline, the place was cleaner than I expected. The bare floorboards were swept twice a day, and there was usually a clothes line of wet underwear stretched across the room. The money obtained from the stolen books was spent on paying the rent (12 guineas a week) or on marijuana.

Marijuana is a non-habit-forming drug that looks like flakes of greeny-brown tea or coarse-grained pepper. If you have contacts you can buy it easily in Soho. It is mixed with tobacco, rolled in brown cigar paper, and often passed from hand-to-hand like the pipe of a hookah. For ten shillings the beat can buy enough "tea" to get high. It produces a sensation like rising up a narrow chimney and hovering high in the air. The body becomes heavy and everything happens in slow motion. The English beats are fond of preluding, the stimulant that has the opposite effect to marijuana. These "slimming tablets" destroy the desire to eat and produce an extraordinary mental brilliance; many beat poets write their poetry with the use of Preludin. The result is work of great sensitivity and strangeness, but with no thought of coherency.

But beat philosophy is not merely drug-taking and sexual promiscuity. The founder of the beat generation in America was Jack Kerouac whose novel *On the Road* started it all. According to Kerouac, beat does not mean "down and out"; it's derived from "beatific" and refers to sainthood. The beats are devoted to the Eastern religion Zen, which believes that the way to achieve sainthood and "enlightenment" is to give the instincts full play. At the moment there are four great centres of beat philosophy in England: Soho, Hampstead, Chelsea and Oxford. The beats from Oxford are likely to turn up in the rooms of their friends in London, and sleep the night on the floor or share marijuana cigarettes. And the Soho and Chelsea types often descend on Oxford. The University authorities regard the whole movement without favour.

The beats have their own terminology. The males are known as beatniks, the females as beat-chicks. You call everybody "man" although the women are sometimes addressed as "kid". There are two types of beatniks: the "wild cat" and the "cool cat". The beats I have described above are typical of the wild cat. They believe in complete self-expression, in doing anything that comes into your head, from turning somersaults in the street to jiving to two different jazz records played at the

'My Night With the Beatniks'

same time. The cool cat tends to spend his time alone. He spends a great deal of time sitting cross-legged and staring at the wall as he tries to get the "true source of inspiration in himself". He is a mystic whose creed is to "dig" everything, and he is likely to declare that a dustbin is just as beautiful as a tree full of birds.

The beat philosophy is the leftover of the Angry Young Man craze of the 1950s, of which (to our amazement) John Osborne and myself were regarded as the founder members. But it is easier to be beats than to be "angry". To be angry you need something to get excited about. To be beat you only need to sit back and drink your Spanish burgundy and call everyone "man".

I am told that most beatniks end by taking a regular job and getting married. I give the whole craze another three years.

The Other Side of Town

Charles Russell

[Setting: London, mainly Soho, in the 1950s]

Chapter 1

"Take your tongue out of my ear and go back to sleep."
Was I tired.
"Charles sweetie, don't get tough, it's not like you. And you're not on the stage now."
She was so right. I hadn't worked for three months.
"Besides, selfish, I can't sleep, this floor's too hard."
"What do you expect, a soft floor?"
I had slept on plenty in the last month. Some softer than this, but when you've got a girl and you're skint and you want a bit of privacy, well! Blaggers can't be choosers.

The floor was hard, but she felt soft, soft and warm, even though we were half dressed. She pulled the sacks closer around us, pressing her body on mine; our lips met. I soon forgot about the floor, believe me.

Something wet hit me on the neck. I looked up. A grey dawn peeped through what was left of the roof. Another splash hit me. I guessed it was raining. Suddenly my guts started rumbling. Making love always makes me feel hungry. So I tied my shoelaces and got up and took my coat off the bed. Geraldine had gone to sleep, a contented smile on her face. Laying there with her long red hair all straggly, she looked like one of her own messy modern paintings.

I picked my way between the rubble on the floor and left, putting some bricks in front of the door just to keep prowlers away. I left her to it. We'd found this place at night, but I guessed she'd find her own way out in time for art school.

I was cold and the drizzle didn't cheer me up. I looked along the alley hoping to see a milk bottle on one of the door steps. The café opposite me had a sack in front of it. I untied it and looked inside. It was full of rolls. I stuffed some under my coat and scouted along the sheltering doorways and collected a bottle of milk.

Rain started to pour down, so I sheltered in the entrance to a warehouse. A few char-looking women hurried by. I supposed the time was about 7 am. My guts rumbled again, and not wanting to eat in the open, I squeezed through a gap in the folding doors.

There were sheets of brown paper everywhere, thousands of them. It must have been a brown paper warehouse. I put my rolls and milk down, shook the rain from my coat and sat on a heap of the brown paper. It groaned and I jumped off it quick. It groaned again and turned over slowly. An unshaven face came out of one end and said:

"What's going on in my bedroom?"
I recognised the bearded figure. I said:

"Do you remember me? I met you in the Alex Café last week. You were sketching a lesbian. She had the longest nose I'd ever seen."

He blinked, mumbled, "Oh, it's only you," and went back to sleep. I recalled that evening when I'd wandered lonely and hungry into that Soho basement Café. It looked so disreputable that I thought my last shilling might get good value there. In its dimly lit wooden floored and tabled interior the customers would have looked out of place anywhere else. Dressed almost in rags, long haired, unshaven men and straggly haired girls, were talking, laughing, even singing in a completely uninhibited manner over their cups of tea and occasional plates of spaghetti. I'd complimented Mike's drawing. He'd stroked his beard and said, "Yes, it's my qualification for membership here. I'm a fucking genius."

He showed me his folder full of sketches and explained that he executes 'Portraits' in pubs and cafes. 'Masterpieces' for a few paltry shillings. He looked about 35. He'd lost some of his wavy black hair and some teeth. And here he was in a brown paper bed with his folder of sketches for a pillow. I shook him awake again.

"Would you like to share my breakfast?"

I showed him the rolls and milk. He woke up like a shot.

"You're a genius," he exclaimed, "I can save my one remaining indigestion tablet for later."

He grabbed a roll and bit fiercely into it.

"It's hard on my remaining teeth," he joked, "Pity you couldn't have made it ham and eggs."

"Sorry," I answered, "Cook's out shopping. It's only fourteen shopping days to Christmas."

We tucked in.

"What's 'The Strength'[1] Mike?" I asked.

He rummaged in the lining of his old furry coat and produced 9d.

"I've got 1/6d,"[2] I said, "It was given to me by some joker in a pub last night to have my hair cut with."

"That's one advantage of having long hair," he said. Then as an afterthought, he added, "I've got a couple of dog-ends."

We talked over our plans for the day. With the 2/3d, we agreed to nip over to the Tube Station for a wash and shave, then I suggested a visit to the National Gallery as it was a good place

---

[1] Money available to spend. Ed.

[2] One shilling and sixpence (decimal equivalent: 7½ pence). Ed.

for loaded tourists. I stood up, brushing the crumbs from my jacket, while Mike put on his shoes and straightened his scarf. We tidied the brown paper and strolled out into Oxford Street.

"This rain might grow some hair on you," I quipped, "let's step into this doorway and smoke your dog-ends, I've some papers and a match book."

We were both wide awake now and enjoyed our quiet smoke in the shelter of a doorway. We amused ourselves calling to the workers hurrying past:

"Get a move on, the boss is waiting. Hurry though you hate it!" etc.

As we reached the Tottenham Court Road toilet I saw a clock. It was 6.30.

"Good morning Doctor," I greeted the toilet attendant, "Two towels and a sharp razor, please."
I put down a 1/- piece.

"Is your mate shaving his beard off?" he asked cheerfully.

"I haven't the energy," Mike replied. He tapped me on the arm, "Don't look now, but who is the elegant gentleman with the drain-pipe trousers and frock coat, carefully adjusting his cravat in the mirror?"

"Ricky!" I exclaimed, "Haven't seen you for days. Have you been eating?"
He turned.

"Good morning to you both. God I feel terrible, I haven't eaten for three days and my collar's been reversed at least five times this week. How do I look?"

"Like the genius poet you are," I said.
Mike, washing his ears, laughed.

"That's good, 'genius' poet, that's *very* good, Ha Ha!"
Ricky ignored this.

"I see you two are in good form today. *You* must have Eaten."

"Not yet, Ricky," I lied, so as not to upset him.

I took off my jacket, turned on the taps and started to wash.

"Come and have a cup of tea with us after," I offered.

"That's wonderful," he replied, "Just wait until I've finished my hair."

"That," said Mike, who was drying himself, "will give you time to shave, Charles."

"You wouldn't have a comb I suppose?" Ricky asked.

"It's among the pencils in my coat pocket," Mike said, "Damn this razor, it's chopped a piece off my moustache."

"I've written just the poem for that," said Ricky, dropping the pencils and comb into a sink, "Listen to this..." He lifted a hand for silence and recited solemnly:

"Living in lovers, lips to feet,
Tenderly clasping from each to each.
Nothing so cutting, nothing so shorn,
Time to remember, sunset to dawn."

Mike and me and the washroom attendant clapped loudly. Someone in a toilet blew a raspberry.

"Ignorant peasant," Ricky expostulated. Then to us: "It's a little thing I tossed off on the back of a Lyons menu card. Do you like it?"

"Magnificent," Mike said, "Inspired, beautiful, brilliant, but, just a detail...What does it mean?"

Ricky drew himself up to his full 5' 8", his cherubic face disdainfully balanced on his left forefinger:

"The meaning doesn't matter. It's the *feeling* here,"— clutching at his lapels, "the feeling *here*,"— clutching at his forehead.

"The only feeling you have is here," said Mike and slapped him daintily on the bottom.

I started to shave.

"Hope that razor's still sharp enough for your barbed wire," said Mike.

When I'd finished and dried, Ricky was still fixing his long blond hair. Mike took Ricky's collar off and, using it as a copy, cut him a new one from a sheet of drawing paper.

"A little more cut away," Ricky demanded, "I must be in the fashion."

"How vain can he get?" Mike asked me and wrote inside it—'With love to Lord Bryon, An Admirer.' Then taking the comb Mike started combing his hair; whilst Ricky struggled to get the collar into position without displacing his.

Eventually he tied his cravat and at last we were ready. We trouped up the steps into the street, in single file, keeping in step to Mike's marching orders:

"Left, right, left, right," he barked, like a pompous Sergeant Major. We reached the corner of Compton Street.

"Let's have tea in 'The French'," I suggested.

We entered, and a hoarse French/Cockney voice greeted us with the challenge: "*En garde!*" It was Pierre, the bogus Count. He was brandishing a rapier, looking as if he had stepped out of *The Three Musketeers*. He thrust through a doughnut with the rapier.

"Ricky *mon ami*," he said, "*accepta vous un bun.*"

Pierre whisked the pierced doughnut over the heads of the few red-eyed unslept characters who sat, drowsy and indifferent, at the tables of the narrow café.

We sat down at the counter ignoring him. I ordered three teas. Pierre was not to be discouraged. Still waving the rapier he said, "This morning, I am to fight a duel. It is, of course, a question of honour. I shall probably be mortally wounded, so I need a witness standing by. Would either of you two gentlemen care to be at my disposal?"

We kept silent. One of the red-eyed characters quietly unhooked the doughnut and started eating it. Pierre was too busy posing to notice.

"All I ask is to be buried in Soho Square," he said, "no flowers please, only a modest headstone inscribed 'Here lies the noble Count Pierre, greatest swordsman of all time. Feared and outcast by a jealous world. Honour Above All'."

Mike spluttered into his tea. We all knew Pierre. He was always like this. He never stopped talking.

"I was invited by Douglas Fairbanks Junior to Warner Brothers film studios yesterday," he continued, "Fairbanks said to me 'Pierre I would like to have you in my next picture, you are the greatest swordsman I have ever met, but you would show me up; I am afraid you are too good for me.' So he turned me down, I was too good for him!" He shrugged his shoulders expressively.

He would have gone on talking for hours, so Mike pushed past him saying, "If you survive your duel Pierre, see you again later."

"No, not tonight," he replied sadly, "I have a temporary job sorting letters for the GPO."

Chapter 2

The sun had broken through now and as we got to Trafalgar Square, the fountains were spraying and the pigeons were looking for their breakfast. We paused on the Gallery steps. Mike opened his folder, took out one of the portraits he carried, and on the back of it began to sketch the scene. Ricky and I left him to it. We pushed our way through the swing doors marked 'Exit Only'.

"I should like to see the Caravaggio, Charles. It always inspires me: 'A thing of beauty is a joy forever'," he quoted. We went to Room 4 and occupied the two imitation Hepplewhite chairs.

"Isn't it marvellous?" he enthused, "I feel I want to absorb every brush stroke."

He was gazing distractedly at his reflection in the glass and pushed a stray lock of hair into place.

"Okay Ricky. I'll have a stroll around. Back in ten minutes if I don't have any luck."

"*Bon chance*," he muttered as I left.

It was like old times being skint in the Gallery. I remembered the Sunday afternoon a couple of months before when I had been homeless and without money. I'd met some middle-aged monster with a maisonette in Lancaster Gate. I moved in with her but the strain of keeping her at arms-length and taking a bath every morning was too much for me and I left. At that time Mac, an artist friend, had organized a holidaying Austrian girl who paid the rent for a studio near the British Museum. She just loved anything in trousers. After a week Mac was a shadow of himself, so I posed as a Secret Service Agent, visited them and told her to leave town immediately because Mac was a suspected Russian spy. She left and we shared the Studio, putting up all the homeless characters we met until the advanced rent ran out. The housekeeper was very glad to get rid of us. Ricky by that time was 'pearl diving'[3] at the 'Shangri-La' in Greek Street. He was eating regularly and sleeping on the premises.

"I feel so virile these days," he had complained, "I simply can't write poetry anymore."

Last week he decided he couldn't stand it any longer, although he still slept in the restaurant, unbeknown to the Manager.

Today was my 'return' to the Gallery. As I walked through the Claude Room, an aroma of cooking filtered up from the kitchen. I quickly moved to the Titian and Rubens Room. There was Mike silently approaching a smartly dressed girl of about 20 who stood in front of Van Dyke's 'Charles the First on Horseback'. I sidled up and heard him start pattering.

"Van Dick was a great artist don't you think?" he said. She turned and smiled.

"Yeah, I sure think he looks wonderful riding that horse." Mike ignored this and continued, "I'm an artist too, of course," shifting his folder into view, 'I haven't brought my horse; but I've a few masterpieces in here." He patted the folder significantly. "I presume you are an American cousin visiting our Gallery?"

"Sure am!" she answered, intrigued.

"I also perceive," he continued, "that you appreciate art. I would be honoured to show you my work and perhaps be permitted to do a sketch of you as a souvenir."

"Go right ahead," she said, flattered.

"But not here!" Mike was shocked, "These masterpieces on the walls are too overpowering. If you would care to accompany me around the Gallery I will relate information about the Masters and afterward conduct you to a nearby Bohemian café for refreshment."

---

[3] Dish-washing. Ed.

She looked thrilled at this. As they strolled away out of earshot Mike took her hand. I knew then that his lunch was assured. I saw a tall skinny long-nosed bespectacled attendant leering across at them. I went into the Rembrandt Room and stood looking at a 'Self Portrait'. Then Ricky came in.

"Just seen Mike walking out with a wonderful girl," he said, "He's lucky. My solitude was disturbed by an ancient hag and," he whispered, "she's following me now."

"Be brave," I told him, "it may be your lunch you know. You don't *have* to go to bed with it."

Ricky was undecided.

"It's in the cause of art," I persuaded.

He sighed, "I'll try, but I'm sure Shelley wouldn't approve. How about you moving in Charles?"

"No offence," I answered quickly, "but it's nearly the office girls' lunch time; I'll feel more confident with them as I'm rather out of practice."

He sighed as he strolled around looking at the Rembrandts. His 'Vulture Woman' appeared and started creeping after him, her mothering instinct fully aroused. I hoped she wouldn't offer him money. He'd refuse it on principle. He always did.

I was feeling drowsy, so I took a seat and must have dozed. Paddy, one of the friendly attendants was shaking my shoulder: "Wake up my bhoy."

I woke up, "Sorry Paddy, I was having a séance."

Then I felt hungry again. I wandered out to the entrance hall and looked dazedly at the clock, it was 2pm. The leering Cyrano-nosed attendant was standing there, still leering, "Lazy Bugger…why don't you get a job?" he mumbled.

I stuck two fingers up at him and pushed myself through the door. Rain was pouring down outside and there were about thirty people standing in the shelter of the porch. I noticed a fair-haired chubby-bottomed Swiss-looking girl on my left.

"I expect you are used to more water than this in Holland," I ventured.

"I don't know, I'm from Switzerland," she said.

"What a coincidence," I replied, "I have a college chum staying there. He enthuses over Swiss hospitality."

She looked pleased, so I talked on about my mythical chum and explained that I had just come back from Paris that morning and was expecting some cash to arrive from Daddy at my Bank. Her name was Elsa, she told me, and she'd just finished a year of looking after children for a family in the wilds of Kent. She'd had a very lonely time of it explaining that domestic service was the only work a foreign girl was allowed to do in England. I sympathised and suggested she accompany me to lunch after visiting my Bank. She came. We went to the first I saw and, while she stood in the doorway, I enquired about changing some foreign coins. The clerk, of course, explained he couldn't do it. So I returned and told her the money had not arrived, which was a shame as I was feeling hungry and had promised to take her to lunch. So she suggested taking *me* to lunch. With a show of reluctance I accepted. We went to Lyons where I gorged myself. Afterwards she left to book in at a hostel in Kensington. She gave me 10/- for expenses and we arranged to meet the following day to celebrate on my allowance. Where?...I didn't bother to remember.

Chapter 3

It was 5.30pm now, so feeling wealthy I took a bus to the Bohemians favourite pub; The Wheatsheaf in Charlotte Street, Soho. After ordering a glass of bitter I sat beside Ironfoot Jack, the only other customer this early. He had a pile of clutter[4] in an open cloth on a newspaper in front of him.

"Ullo!' he said, "jest makin' sum earrings fer me stall." His pliers nipped a length off a coil of gold wire, then he strung a few beads on it and twisted it over the ear-holding piece.

"Will they sell?" I enquired.

"Course," he whispered confidingly, "they're genu-wine han-tiques."

In a manner of speaking, Ironfoot Jack was 'King of the Bohemians' in Soho. As a lad he'd lived with gypsies. In his youth he had worked all kind of side shows and spectacles, many of them original, in circuses all over the country. In the 20s he opened five clubs in Soho. Unfortunately for him one was raided by the police and after his two year sentence in Reading jail he founded a religion: 'Children of the Sun'. He looked very imposing in his robes in the photo he showed me, his thick-set powerful head offset by his iron foot, which replaced the lower half of his left leg. He took off his black trilby hat and unwound his hair which he never cut—it reached below his shoulders.

"Ow's yer luck these days?" he asked.

"It just isn't," I replied.

"Not doin anyfin in the fee-ater world these days then?"

"Given me up," I answered.

"Why don't yer busk a queue?" he suggested.

"Busk a queue?" I exclaimed.

"Yers, give ten minutes of Shakespeare outside a classical show, then go round with the 'Bottle'."

"Bottle?" I asked.

"The collecshun," he explained.

I looked at Jack's paper.

---

[4] Street trader's term for a jumbled collection of items, mostly useless, but still considered saleable. Ed.

"What time is it?" I called to Arthur behind the bar. "6.30," he answered.

I read in the paper that Shaw's *Man and Superman* went on at the New Theatre, St. Martin's Lane at 7.30. If I hurried I could be there in time.

"I'll have a try," I said.

"Good lad," Jack was pleased, "Ere," he said, "I've folded this paper fer yer to collect in."

I thanked him, gulped down my beer and walked quickly through the back streets into Tottenham Court Road and jumped onto a passing bus.

When I saw the queue at St. Martin's Court, about forty pairs deep, my courage dropped, but I clenched my fists, strode forward and faced the middle of the queue. I raised both arms, took a deep breath and yelled louder than I had expected to:

"Ladies and Gentlemen, good evening! In the short time you have left before going into the theatre, I shall endeavour to entertain you with excerpts from the classical repertoire."

Everybody was quiet. They were probably shocked. I waited for laughter or comments—none came. I recited the Agincourt speech from *Henry V*, starting slowly and quietly:

"Once more unto the breach dear friends, once more," I felt the people were sympathetic. My speech got more enthusiastic, more forceful. I felt the crowd was with me. On the last line: "Cry God for Harry, England, and Saint George!" someone clapped, then another, then another. My throat felt dry and a tear threatened to trickle down, so I quickly continued with T S. Eliot's 'Preludes'. Then I declared loudly:

"During the next item from Shakespeare's 'Sonnets', I will pass among you with the Box Office, so now may I say thank you, thank you all so very much for your wonderful reception here tonight."

The Other Side of Town

As I walked among the queue collecting coins and reciting, I remembered what the divine Sarah Bernhardt had said: "Give me four boards and a passion and I can act." The queue was moving in now and soon it had gone. I stood with a newspaper full of coins in my hand feeling I had lost a host of friends.

I felt a hand on my shoulder.

"Charles, you were great," a voice said sincerely, "you must recite some of *my* poems next time."
It was Ricky with Mike behind him waving a sketch.

"This is how you looked," he said, "like an old ham."

"Ironfoot told us at The Wheatsheaf where you were, so we came to see your opening night,' Ricky added.

"Well," I said a little dazed, "Let's celebrate in this pub on the corner. Glasses of beer on the takings."
Arm-in-arm they danced me into the saloon. It was The Round Table pub in St. Martin's Lane.

"Three glasses of bitter," I called over to the barman.

"That'll be 2/3d," he said.

"How's your ulcer, Mike?" I enquired, "will it absorb some beer?"

"It's O.K," he replied, grabbing a jug.
As I counted out the price in pennies and small change on the counter, Mike and Ricky told me of their day's adventures. Ricky had been treated to lunch after which the Vulture offered him a pound note. He refused it, as usual with money, and stamping his foot in a huff, left her immediately. Mike related that he had sold a portrait of his American girl to her for 10/- after lunch. So there we were all happy and quietly sipping our beer. Mike spotted a vacant chair at a table, walked over, sat down, took out his pipe and lit it, laying his folder in front of him on the table.

Suddenly the two beers Ricky and I had been drinking were snatched off the counter by a man who introduced himself curtly:

"I am the Manager, you can't drink here; do you mind leaving." We were amazed.

"Why?" we asked.

"I'm not giving a reason," he said brusquely, "just leave!"

"We're not going until we've our finished beer," I said. The Manager looked menacing and beckoned to the barman. Ricky almost exploded with indignation.

"I'm going to fetch a policeman," he said, and rushed out.

Mike saw him go and called over, "What's happening?"

I walked over quickly and told him. The Manager followed close behind.

"He's your friend is he?" said the Manager to Mike, "then I must ask you to leave as well."

By now the other customers in the Saloon were interested in what was going on, and stood quietly watching. Mike was adamant, "I have bought a glass of beer, and I'm drinking a glass of beer and I'm not going until I'm ready," he spoke calmly, but his Scots dialect showed through his precise English, "Incidentally," he added, "this is a damned outrage!"

He grasped his mug of beer firmly with both hands. The barman arrived and tried to tip Mike out of his chair. Mike tossed the beer straight into his fat face. Spluttering, he stepped back. I tripped him and he went sprawling. The Manager turned to grab me. Mike leapt up and jabbed him in the belly with his folder. The drawings went flying all over the floor. The two of us stood firmly in front of the door. Mike addressed the customers in a loud voice.

"You gazers, with your smug expressions, don't you realise that human rights and freedom are being mocked?"

There was no reply. Someone sniggered. Mike tried again, "Is this your idea of fair play? You hypocritical cowards!"

Still no answer.

"Mike old boy," I said gently, "to these people we are just funnily dressed, long haired tramps. They don't care if we are pushed around. They can't be bothered with anything they haven't been conditioned for by schooling, television or the popular press."

I helped Mike to pick up his drawings in the silence. Then I opened the door and followed him out. There we stood just thinking to ourselves for a long minute. Ricky arrived with his policeman who opened a door and called the Manager outside.

"What's all the trouble Sir?" he asked, very officially, notebook and pencil at the ready.

"I don't want these types on my premises," the Manager said. That was all he said and the policeman was satisfied. The three of us, outcast and silent, walked dejectedly through the Seven Dials on our way home to Soho. The lamp lights in Soho Square looked like little candles in the foggy air as we passed them. We felt a little chilly and in our own particular ways a little lonely. Charlotte Street was dark and deserted looking as we approached it. A couple of hours in the company of which we were part of was what we needed.

Chapter 4

At a table in the Alex Café, Palma strummed gently on his guitar, while an unshaven lad in a raincoat explored the ashtrays for cigarette ends. Palma strummed so quietly that I heard the hailstones rattling on the windows. Above the table where Ricky and I sat with two cups of tea gone cold, a few strings of coloured paper dangled from the ceiling. They reminded me that Christmas was coming. About this time next week, outside people would be gorging their turkey dinners in comfortable homes in front of blazing fires.

The Alex's half dozen or-so tables were also furnished with cold cups of tea. Most of them were ordered hours before. Across the room from me Iron Foot Jack was explaining to Pierre, the swordsman/postman, that times were different for Bohemians twenty years ago. His black cloak and inevitable high-collared cravat gave him the air of a Mephisthophelian Santa Claus.

"A dozen cracked eggs for tuppence," he was saying, "a penny piece of cheese and a piece of bread and you 'ad a banquet. A crowd of us would get together at my gaff in Charlotte Street and have a feast to the 'Sun God'."

He lifted his black trilby hat and waved it to emphasize his meaning.

"Rent for the basement was 5-bob[5] a week and there was plenty of room to put up those who were 'on the floor'. No derelicts, layabouts or bums, mind, 'cos this was a respectable gaff, for the enlightened." He waved his hat descriptively, "A flaming brazier lit up the altar and the pictures and tapestries which adorned the walls. There were plenty of cushions all over the floor for comfort, and music was provided by a little geezer what played the mouth organ." He paused to replace his hat, "Pity the law didn't understand the nude dancing rituals," he reminisced, "that's what got me lumbered in jail for two years."

---

[5] 5 shillings (25p). Ed.

He leaned back gazing vacantly at the ceiling with its strings of dangling coloured paper.

"There were hundreds of Bohemians about then. The necessities of life were easy to get. Nowadays there are only a few 'free spirits' left. So called Society 'as made life a financial problem." He sipped at his cold tea, "Operating capital gets scarcer and scarcer."

Pierre broke in with a verbal flourish, "But of course, we 'ad ze revolution in France and gave to Society ze guillotine. After zat everyone was on ze floor!"

At their adjoining table, a huddled old man, with long white hair straggling over his tightly buttoned coat collar, chuckled wheezily and turned over a page from a pile of tattered books. A piece of cardboard propped on the table in front of him was inscribed 'Ernest Page—Astrologer—Predictions 1/6d.' He turned to the couple at the table next to him, "It's all in the stars," he stated sagely, "I'll do you and your lady friend for only 1/6d the two."

"Do me a favour Dad," replied the youth he had addressed who looked very emaciated with his close-cropped ginger hair, "do me a favour and tell me," he leaned nearer, "do they smoke 'The Weed' on Jupiter?"

He took a long pull at his rolled up cigarette and passed it to his lady friend.

"Ssh!" she whispered loudly, "even the walls 'ave ears." She was wearing enough black for a funeral, I noticed.

"He's joking of course," she told Ernest and smiled weakly without taking the roll-up from her unpainted lips.

Ricky, who was contemplating his half empty tea cup, murmured in my ear, "Ginger's high. He sold me couple of sticks on credit just before you came in."

The Other Side of Town

Then Michael, the proprietor, called, "Any-a-one vant a teas?"

His body was so short his bald head barely reached above the counter.

"All right," I called back, "how about you putta some hot water in these two. And bring us a cheese roll?"

He looked surprised about the cheese roll, so I waved a 1/- piece to reassure him. He came over, collected the cups of cold tea and returned to his vanishing point behind the counter. Palma strummed a loud chord on his guitar.

"Ah AH AH AH AH AH," he sang going up and down the scale.

"No noises please!" Michael called plaintively.

"Noise?" he answered indignantly, "it's music. One day when I sing like Caruso did, it will cost five guineas to listen from so near."

Ricky murmured in my ear, "Michael will be dead if he waits that long". Then aloud to Palma he said,"How are your studies getting along Maestro?"

"Don't have much time to practice these days," Palma replied sadly, "I'm too busy doing the pubs, pushing the door open with my foot and singing popular rubbish for the peasants."

"Tell me Palma," I said, "why do they call you Palma?"

He considered for a minute, "I used to be a pickpocket," he admitted and he started strumming again, "Then I found my golden voice," he explained.

"What a pity," Ricky whispered.

"Right now," Palma continued, "my voice doesn't sound so good, but neither did Caruso's when he started. Like the wind in the shutters, people said. You wait till I've practiced some more, then you'll see."

He tucked his brightly coloured scarf into the collar of his old astrakhan coat, "It must be nearly 9 o'clock," he said, then louder, "Any of you bums got a watch?"
No one answered.

"Well it's time to visit the pubs. Pity it's so cold, it's difficult to play the guitar with frozen fingers."
Michael brought over the teas and the cheese roll, scowled at Palma strutting out and returned to his counter.

"Have you seen Mike today?" I asked, "I was sleeping this morning in the Reading Room at South Africa House. I didn't wake up till 4, then I came straight here."

"I haven't seen him for nearly a week," Ricky replied.

"He's gone all suburban since he moved to Camden Town. I believe he's been lumbering girls from the galleries during the day and sketching portraits in the pubs during the evenings. I haven't been around myself much before ten as I've been doing theatre queues with Thespy. We do the quarrel scene from *Julius Caesar* and Shylock and Antonio on the Rialto from *The Merchant of Venice*. Thespy's always drunk which makes the performance rather difficult. Sometimes he forgets himself and swears at the audience. And how are you enjoying life at Hampstead?"

"It's very arty up there you know. The pubs are full of after office hours 'Bohemians' whose starched collars show beneath their woolly sweaters. They are so bogus they bore me to death."

"Is the girl still keeping you happy?" I asked.

"She's so materialistic," he said with a sigh, "she doesn't seem content to have a wonderful spiritual relationship. She's always after my body."

"That surprises me," I replied, "Surely as she's on the game, her customers satisfy her physical needs?"

43

"She's got some silly idea that I don't love her unless I make love to her," he explained adding, "women are always after the one thing."

"Yes," I agreed, "isn't it terrible!"

Ricky sighed again and sipped his tea distractedly. He pulled a sheaf of toilet paper from his pocket and handed it to me.

"What do you think of my 'Ode to a Silent Lark'?" he asked, "Please excuse the paper, but I was inspired at an awkward moment."

I looked at the Ode. As usual his writing was illegible. I returned it to him.

"You must read it to me yourself," I said, "when we are in more sympathetic surroundings."

Ricky was eyeing the cheese roll with interest.

"May I have a piece?" he asked, "I'm feeling rather hungry."

"Of course," I said and passed him the plate.

"Thank you Charles," he said, "by way of repayment, if you would care to join me afterwards, I know a place where we can smoke two sticks of charge in private."

I looked across involuntarily at emaciated ginger hair. He was drawing fiercely at another cigarette, his girlfriend huddled closely to him, all glassy-eyed and ecstatic.

Ricky and I finished our roll and teas. We walked to the counter. I gave Michael 1/- and carefully counted his change. As we passed through the door two girls came in arm-in-arm. One wore a man's belted raincoat, a trilby hat and smoked a pipe.

I followed Ricky down the street towards Soho Square, the hail and icy wind making us hurry.

Chapter 5

Ricky led me over the Charing Cross Road to a derelict alleyway called Pheonix Street. There, following him, I clambered over a wall and through a window, reaching what had been the first floor front room of a house. There, on some dust covered boxes in the corner, we sat down gingerly. Ricky produced his two reefers. I lit them with a book match.

"I hope you'll excuse the precautions Charles, but one has to be careful about smoking this stuff."

"This is good," I said inhaling, "I feel great."
Ricky smoked greedily.

"I'm flying," he said, "flying high above the roof."
I felt I was on a magic carpet too.

"I'm drifting over London," I said, "doesn't it look small?"

"Yes," he agreed, "let's drift to Africa where it's warm."

"Look out!" I shouted, "we've nearly hit the Eiffel Tower!"

"Bail out, bail out," he yelled, "we've sprung a leak!"
At that moment, a tall shadow appeared in the doorway and a booming voice cried out:

"I'm King Pharaoh. What infidels are ye who trespass in my sacred halls?"
Was this apparition real or a result of the hashish cigarette?
The voice continued, "Tongues of fire aloft warned me of your presence. Speak!"
Ricky broke what seemed to be a very long silence:

"It's me, Ricky. I'm having a smoke with a friend."
The figure peered closer at us. From the grimy window the street lamp's glow etched his features in bold relief. They were very dignified. Lean with an aquiline nose and dark piercing eyes,

which reflected brightly from under a tall wide-brimmed hat. His beard was very long and pointed. I guessed his age at around 30. The unkempt figure laughed loudly, exposing rows of blackened teeth.

"Ricky!" he exclaimed, "I mistook you for spies from the Pharisees come to depose me." He sniffed enquiringly, "Hashish," he said and laughed again, "Might I partake of the weed?" he asked with great condescension.

Ricky gave him what was left of his cigarette. The Pharaoh inhaled.

"Very invigorating," he murmured "very invigor-ating."

I handed Ricky what was left of my cigarette.

"This is Charles," he said standing up to introduce me.

I stood up too. The Pharaoh drew a long bony hand from the sleeve of his shabby coat.

"Welcome friends," he said, "come to my chamber and I shall show you 'Corn in Egypt'."

He turned abruptly and vanished through the doorway into the darkness. I went over to Ricky who was standing by the window.

"Who was that?" I asked incredulously.

"He believes he's Pharaoh King of Egypt sent here in exile. He's usually out at this hour," he explained, "we'd better go upstairs to his chamber, or else he'll be offended. I know the way, follow me."

Ricky led me up the creaky stairs to the attic. King Pharaoh was reclining on a heap of pungent straw. He picked up a handful as we entered and strewed it across the floor.

"Here it is," he chuckled "Corn in Egypt, Corn in Egypt. I collected it from Covent Garden Market this morning with some fruit and veg."

I hoped he wouldn't set fire to anything as a candle burned on a fruit box in the corner. Cardboard was fixed across the windows to keep the light from showing outside, I presumed, and also to keep the cold out. While I noticed these things the Pharaoh was talking confidingly to Ricky.

"Why not move into my Palace here?" he offered, "there are plenty of spare rooms and the corn makes a bed fit for a King," he chuckled at his joke.

"That's very generous of you," Ricky answered seriously, "but I have a room in Hampstead now."

"Hampstead," he shuddered, "a room! Why live with the Pharisees in their slave's world. Here you can live like a King. No one to bother you and tell you what to do, no rent to pay and no one to impress. Food from the market and money from loyal subjects at every street corner."

"It's a very attractive life," Ricky agreed, "but I haven't got the character to be a King."
He shook hands with the Pharaoh.

"We must be going," he said, "I must get back to Hampstead."

"You have lost your freedom," the Pharaoh said, "but remember you're welcome any time and bring Charles, and perhaps," he added archly, "some more hashish?"
I shook hands with him too, then followed Ricky downstairs.

"Shall I show you out?" the Pharaoh called after us, "I don't keep any servants."

"Thanks, I can find the way," Ricky answered.

We turned left at the first floor, climbed through the window, over the wall again and were back in the Charing Cross Road, amid the shaved and starched crowd leaving the Pheonix Theatre.

"Ricky," I said, "you know the strangest people. Where did you meet that one?"
He thought for a moment, then said:

"Oh, he tapped me for 6d one evening on a street corner."

We walked across to the bus stop while Ricky explained that his girl would be wondering where he was, as she always liked to see him safely indoors before she went out hustling customers in Hyde Park.

"I hope she has a busy night, Ricky, that will give you a chance to work on your 'Ode'."

His 24 bus to Hampstead arrived and he boarded it.

"Give my regards to Mike if you see him," he said.

"I will," I called as the bus moved away. Poor Ricky, I thought. His comfort is costing him a lot. I had met his girl in Soho one evening and had a chat. She told me that when she was 17 her father had raped her, so she had come to London from her home in Manchester feeling her chances for marriage were ruined there. She had hoped to find the luxury in London she felt her attractiveness deserved. But not finding a storybook millionaire she had resorted to 'the Practical thing', as she put it, and sold herself temporarily to anyone. By conventional standards she was very attractive; though a little plump in the chest and hips. She regarded Ricky as a novelty, as he was well aware. Though living outside of society, as he did, she found more happiness with him then with the conventionally prejudiced hypocrites, who though willing to enjoy her, had been educated to regard her with disgust.

Chapter 6

I wandered along the Tottenham Court Road, wondering what to do. The night air was chilly and I only had left 1/- of the 18/- I had collected from Saturday night's queue at the Curzon Cinema. As I passed Goodge Street Station the rattle of a dustbin lid caught my attention. I turned and saw a figure in a coat that reached down to its ankles bent intently over a dustbin. As I got nearer I saw it was a woman and she was probing its depths. I was surprised to see who it was.

"Hello Countess," I said, "Cold tonight eh?"
She straightened up and peered at me shortsightedly.

"Charles my dear, how nice to see you," she waved a hand in greeting, "Yes I am nearly frozen to death, but I can't bear the thought of another night under the stairs in Neal Street. So draughty you know."
I did know. I had tried to spend a night there before I found my concrete floor off Oxford Street. It was the basement of a printing shop which fitted in under the stairs. Many of the Soho characters slept there or tried to. The place stank for one thing, of all sorts of odours. There was no toilet on the premises. The ancient mattresses and sacking that covered the floor were infested with lice, who didn't seem to mind the chill winds that ventilated the place. What with the draughts, the smell, the lice and the noises of snores, ravings and people having all kinds of sex, I too agreed it was better to be outside.

"Besides," the Countess added bravely, "this night air does one good." She pointed at the dustbin, "Nothing of interest here I'm afraid. I'm hoping I may find a blanket of some sort somewhere."

"It must be cold work Countess…I'm on my way to Tony's Café," I lied, "would you like to join me for a cup of tea?"

"Delighted dear boy," she replied, 'When one reaches my age," (she was around 50), "one appreciates the little comforts."

'Well,' I thought, 'there goes my last shilling!'

She adjusted her feathered velvet hat and we strolled arm-in-arm towards Tony's in Warren Street as if we were strolling through the gardens to the Casino at Monte Carlo.

"I am still having difficulties with my legacy," she said by way of conversation, "My son and his wife are living in luxury somewhere in London. Where? I *have* tried to find out, but nobody takes me seriously. All I want is just £2 a week from the family estate, then I shall be off to sunny Spain. There, on two English pounds, one can live comfortably, for a week. I know the country well and can speak the language fluently."
I was surprised at this.

"I know you speak French like a native Countess, but Spanish, really? You surprise me."

"My dear," she said quickly, "I also speak German and Italian fluently...when I was a young girl I travelled extensively in Europe with my family."
She fell silent for a while.

"Here's Tony's," I said, "now we can get warm."
Tony's windows were all steamed over. I followed the Countess inside. The place was crowded. The five or six tables were occupied with taxi drivers, railway porters, drunks and bums. Along the left wall ran a counter. The Countess took the one vacant stool of the row in front of it. Tony sidled over to us. He smiled at the Countess.

"Good evening Madam," he said politely, "*Fi molto freddo ancora Signorina*," he added in Italian.

"Yes Tony, but I'm sure it brings you plenty of customers."

"*Si Signorina*," Tony replied.
I was baffled by all this.

"What did he say Countess?"

"He agreed that the cold weather is good for business, the sly rascal."

"I understand," I said and we laughed, "Oh yes," I called, "Two teas, Tony please. Let's take off your coat Countess, you'll appreciate it more when you go out again."
Underneath she was wearing a plain green dress which was almost obscured with necklaces, bracelets and broaches. One of the five or six bracelets on her left arm, appeared to be made of jade.

"That's a very nice bracelet," I said, touching it.

"Everyone admires it," she answered, "I have promised it to at least ten people so as not to offend them."

Tony brought the tea over. I passed him my shilling and be gave me 4d change from the till. We warmed our hands on the hot cups. I pulled over the sugar bowl.

"Two lumps for me please," she said, "my hands are too frozen to do it."
While we slowly sipped the warming tea I told her about the library at South Africa House and suggested she might like to sleep there.

"Not quite my cup of tea," she replied, "it's a little too public. How's your friend Michael?" she asked, apparently to turn the conversation from her social habits.

"I haven't seen him for a week, ever since he moved to a room somewhere."

"The lucky boy, to have a room in this cold weather. Perhaps he has a wealthy patron, I wouldn't wonder."
The idea amused me and I must have smiled for the Countess added, "He should have a patron, he's a very fine artist and this is a stupid world."

A well-dressed pink-faced man peeped in at the door. He was probably looking for a homeless young boy to take care of.

"Shut that bloody door!" one of the customers called out. Pink-face smiled in an embarrassed way, withdrew himself and closed the door.

As I was nearly at Camden Town I thought I'd call round and see if Mike was at home. I wished the Countess luck, buttoned up my coat and left the 4d on the counter.

"Have another tea on me," I said. I patted her on the shoulder and left.

Chapter 7

I was getting fed up with being reminded of the cold. I hurried along the less windy side turnings behind the Hampstead Road. I asked an Irish layabout at Camden Town crossroads if he knew Delancey Street. He mumbled that he didn't. The drunken bum. The ticket collector in the underground station said he knew the street and explained very clearly how to get there. I followed his directions and arrived about half an hour and a few enquiries later.

It was a street of four-storied houses with railinged basements. Facing the railway cutting was number 54. Distinguishable from the others only by its number. The only light on in the street was at its top window. This, I realized, must be Mike's room. I whistled the opening theme of Beethoven's Fifth Symphony, which was our signal. The window opened and a silhouette waved. Moments later the front door opened and Mike leapt at me grasping my hand and pumped it vigourously.

"Great to see you Charles," he said, "I thought you were dead."

"Nothing so commonplace," I replied, "I've been to Stratford with Thesby for a week, giving some real

Shakespearean performances in that town of commercialised bogusity."

"Great stuff," he said, then putting a finger to his lips, "follow me quietly."

We crept up the lino-covered stairs, so as not to disturb the other tenants. A little out of breath, we reached the top floor and entered Mike's room. He went over to his easel and picked up his pallet and brushes. His wavy black hair was dishevelled and he was wearing only a black shirt and red scarf. I hadn't noticed before, but he was wearing no trousers, or shoes. Apparently he had been busy painting his wild looking reflection from the mantelpiece mirror, for his large canvas was covered in all sorts of ideas. Brilliant patches of colour described his face which appeared to be writhing under a mass of black snakes for hair.

"This is very striking Mike," I said.

"Yes," he replied jabbing fiercely at it with a brush load of lemon yellow, "It's in the descriptive style."

On the table in the centre of the room was a jumble of beer bottles, brushes and opened art books, whose coloured plates were pinned all over the walls. On the floor were old shirts, ties, trousers and jackets. He noticed my perplexed expression.

"No it wasn't a whirlwind. I've been trying on various costumes for this Masterpiece."

He took a draught from one of the bottles, then handed it to me.

"Have a drink Charles and join the party," he waved his disengaged hand outside the circle of light thrown on his easel. My eye caught a brassiere, draped over the back of a chair, together with other feminine garments

"Been trying these on too?" I asked.

He chuckled, busy at his canvas. I looked closer at his single bed and realised there were three half naked girls sleeping on it under the quilt. Mike looked over at my exclamation of surprise.

"Met them in The Wheatsheaf where I was sketching tonight. One's a cracker, the other two are monsters. They told me they were tourists from the provinces, eager for a break from their dull routine lives. So I took them to the 91 Café to see the Bohemians and buy me a chicken supper. Then I tried to lumber the cracker but she wouldn't desert the monsters, so I lumbered the three of them and a crate of booze into a taxi, which they also paid for as an advance on a portrait in triplicate. When we got back here we had a few drinks. I felt inspired so I started this self-portrait and left them to pass out on the kip. I'm glad you dropped in Charles. It'll be a tight squeeze, but we can do it." He handed me the bottle. I took a long drink.

"Okay Mike," I said, "for you I'll make the effort."
I took off my coat and approached the bed. With a quick movement I whipped off the quilt. A pink bottom in a pair of transparent briefs was uppermost. I gave it a friendly smack.

*

A loud burping noise awoke me. It was Mike whose head had somehow got onto my shoulder. I looked at the watch on the wrist which dangled in front of me. It read 12.30. Disentangling my legs from the monster who was lying across them I got up and dressed. The girls were sleeping soundly so I threw some clothes over them to keep them warm and woke Mike.

"Let's go out," I said, "and get some fresh air. If we wake the girls they'll expect us to make love to them again." He dressed quietly and we walked out into another grey day.

Chapter 8

On our way to the corner Mike told me that he had met a weirdy in Lyons Corner House yesterday afternoon who told him he'd received a message from outer space to give his wealth to the artists of this world.

"He said," Mike continued, "that if I met him outside the bank in Tottenham Court Road at 2 o'clock today he'd patronise my art to the tune of £50."

"£50! Was he drunk?"

"Sober as a magistrate," Mike said.

"It sounds crazy," I said.

"That's what I thought," he answered, "Well I've got 3d. Shall we share a bun or speculate it on the bus fare to Mr. Outer Space? Personally I don't think he'll show up."

"A fifty pounds gift from a Lyons customer sounds nutty to me. But take a chance, Mike, you never know, this is Christmas week and he might be Santa Claus."

"I gave up believing in Santa Claus years ago and my guts are dancing a tango. Let's get that bun."

Being skint myself, the bun idea, after the night's exertions, was very tempting. We strolled silently towards a café in Camden High Street. I felt guilty.

"Mike," I said "You must meet that nutter. You'll never forgive yourself if you don't. Guts ache or no guts ache."

So I said cheerio and wished him good luck as he jumped on a bus on his way to the bank date.

Chapter 9

I stood for a moment wondering what to do. I stroked my chin. The stubble wasn't too thick. Then I remembered that a very talkative and boring female had told me she lived in a house near Regents Park, which was nearby, and pressed her address into my pocket one evening in The Wheatsheaf. I'd no intention of calling on her at the time, but now it seemed the only way out. I found the crumpled note with her address and, after about fifteen minutes searching, found the place. I rang the bell of 16b. It was a basement door, in a street of uniform Georgian style mansions. I rang the bell a second time. It was really a chime, one of those two tone, bong-bong noise boxes. A bright-eyed face peered at me through the window curtain. It was the Vulture. A moment later the door was discreetly opened.

"Why hello; you are a surprise," she squawked and primped at golden wisps straggling from under her brightly-coloured headscarf, "Come in; do. Excuse my appearance. Just preparing lunch."

How convenient, I thought.

"I've just eaten," I lied, explaining, "breakfast you know."

She guided me to a settee in a room overcrowded with furniture.

"What a pity," she tutted, "I'm just making a stew. Handy stew, I call it, because it's so handy to prepare."

I laughed in sympathy.

"Very fond of stew myself, Irish descent you know and in any case good manners dictate that I join you."

It didn't fool her for a moment, but she seemed delighted with the patter. She posed for a moment then scuttled to what I imagined was the kitchen. Her front room was very interesting. A clear indication of her character. Bum modernist paintings, cloth dolls from Spain with never used wine skins hanging guiltily beside them. Curios and bric-a-brac were everywhere, except on the table which was laid with doylies for one.

She came back with freshly applied lipstick glistening on her skinny lips. She arranged another place at the table. Then the chimes rang. Her face tightened up.

"Whoever can that be?" she gasped walking briskly to the tiny entrance hall. The latch clicked and I imagined her peeping through the door in that discreet way of hers.

"Gertie dear, just thought I'd drop in for a spot of lunch," a beery male voice boomed, "I hope I'm just in time." The voice and owner came into the room. Six feet of heavily-moustached hail-fellow-well-met, bum-of-the-old-school, eyed the table hungrily. Gertie smiled weakly, knowing she was beaten and introduced us.

"Meet Charles. This is Bill," she searched for a phrase, "An old friend."

I stood up and took his hairy hand. Then Gertie sat him down opposite me in an armchair that seemed to shrink as he overwhelmed it.

"Making a stew," she repeated, "hope there'll be enough for three." He didn't take the hint, the bastard!

"Jolly-dee," he chuckled.

"Jolly-dee," I chuckled back.

What a mean bastard, I thought. I could have willingly stabbed him with the bread knife.

"Charles eh?" he said as if the name was a joke, "and what do you do, old boy?"

I guessed he was some sort of travelling salesman.

"Travelling salesman," I said.

"By Jove what a coincidence!" he chortled, "hey Gertie, why didn't you tell me Charles was a traveller too?"

A laugh from the kitchen was his reward for that one.

"And what do you travel in, eh?" he chuckled.

I resisted the corny answer about women's underwear and answered with a sincerity that surprised me, as by now I really hated him from his fat head downwards, "Please don't let's talk about me. You seem such a very interesting personality. I'm dying to hear about *you*."

That really set him off, the egotistical bore! From the moment Gertie brought the depleted portions of stew to the moment he left, just after the coffee, he talked and talked, pausing only to gulp, swallow or wipe his obscene moustache. I expect he talked about himself, because I wasn't listening. Anyway, he finally left. He also left the washing up, but, believe me, I didn't mind that at all. I wiped the bits of crockery as Gertrude, as I called her for flattery, pulled them from the soapy water with her red rubber-gloved hands.

"Have you ever done any acting Charles?" she asked.

I thought she was about to take the rise out of my patter.

"As a matter of fact," I stated truthfully, "I have. My last show was 'Ace of Clubs', Noel Coward's in the West End."

"I thought you might have because you have a very interesting manner," she said; she seemed serious and didn't seem to be angling with the bodyline either.

We dried our hands, then she showed me the bedroom. It was an elegantly furnished place with long french windows opening onto the garden. She flung her bony form upon the double bed. This, I thought, will require all my courage. I sat beside her and linked her bony hand to mine. She withdrew it coyly.

"Please don't imagine wrong things," she croaked, fluttering hairless eyelids. Did I feel relieved! I stood up quickly.

"Sorry," I said, then, "Let's go for a stroll in the Park. The cold air will calm the desire I have for you."

It'll be safer there, I thought.

"I'll have to change clothes," she said unzipping the side of her gown. I sighed.

"What a pity we've known each other such a short time. I'll wait in the garden."

I passed smartly through the french windows and up the steps to the grassy refuge. She appeared shortly, dressed in trousers and a shabby raincoat belted tightly to give an illusion of shape. The get-up, I presumed, was intended so as not to intimidate me. In fact she looked more skint than I did!

We left via the garden path. Chattering idly about the birds, trees, flowers and other trivia, she minced through Regent's Park as far as the lake before her skinny legs needed relief. I spread my jacket grasswards and we sat. I suppose, I thought, it's time for romance.

"Gertrude," I murmured, "I'm having a wonderful afternoon. You're a very fascinating girl."
That stumped her. She just glued her eyes on the lake and swallowed. I pattered on.

"Could you let me have some bus fare?" I asked, "Mac is meeting me in The Wheatsheaf at 6.30."

"Who's Mac?" she asked, "a girl friend?"

"Heavens no!" I threw up shocked hands, "Mac's a stocky, grizzly-haired, foghorn-voiced genius of an actor."
She dug into a pocket and came up with 2/6d, which she handed me.

"Tonight we are busking the New Theatre and perhaps the Empire, Leicester Square. It's offering an intelligent film for a change," I explained, "so the audience should appreciate us."

"I didn't know you were a busker," she said.

"One has to use what one has, in this world," I answered archly, "half-crowns[6] from kind ladies, hardly keep one in the style to which one is not accustomed."

---

[6] 'half crown' was the name of a 2/6d piece (decimal equivalent 12½p). Ed.

I kissed her lightly on the cheek, thanked her for lunch, promised to phone soon, and ran off.

Chapter 10

Leaving the park I jumped into a bus at Baker Street. It had just pulled up at a five-yard-long queue of office workers. When the bus halted at the official stop, the respectable looking people kicked, nudged and screamed at each other trying to get on first. But apart from the exercise value, their efforts were wasted. I'd got the last empty seat.

With the traffic jams in Oxford Street, I reached The Wheatsheaf later than I'd expected. Pushing open the door I espied Mac at the far end of the bar.

"Are you getting drunk already?" I said.

Chapter 11

"Right on time Laddie!" he barked gruffly, pointing a silver-topped walking stick at the clock. Mac looked different somehow. He must have realised my bewilderment for he laughed, barking like the wire-haired terrier he resembled. He rubbed his chin with a grand gesture.

"Shaved off the whiskers, Laddie. I'm not King Lear nay more this season and besides one has got to keep one's national character at all costs," he waved his stick descriptively, "though this Sceptered Isle of ours seems kinder today to the strangers within its gates." He hung his head regretfully, "Another pint of bitter," he growled at the barman, "And what's for you?" he yelled at me, rolling his eyes.

"The pint you just ordered," I replied.
Mac was swaying gently. I leaned over to Arthur the barman.

"How much of this stuff has he poured into his guts this last half hour?" I asked.

Arthur hesitated, "About five pints. Oh…and one whiskey chaser—on the house."

He reluctantly put the pint Mac ordered on the counter. I picked it up.

"I think I'd better have this," I gave him 2/- and got the change.

"Don't get sloshed Mac," I pleaded, "we're working this evening."

"I know Laddie," he agreed, "but I've been rehearsing to these patrons," he spat the word, "whose alcoholic contributions have been gratefully accepted."

He bowed grandly to his audience of four stiff collared admirers who sat enchanted; at a safe distance.

"Come on Mac. Curtain up in fifteen minutes," I finished the pint.

"Just time for one more," he barked, "barman!"

Another voice broke in behind us.

"Who are these uncouth layabouts?" it enquired. I turned and saw an elegant grey suit, brown suede shoes, white shirt, silk tie and a carnation buttonhole. I couldn't believe my eyes. It was Mike.

"Three scotches with soda on the side," he ordered. Mac was as surprised as I was, "What, has this thing appeared again tonight?" he quoted.

"Your bare chin looks indecent," Mike chided him, "careful you're not arrested for exposing yourself."

Arthur brought over the drinks.

"Have a drink yourself and get this framed," he flashed a five-pound note in front of Arthur's incredulous gaze.

"It's the finest picture I've seen since the Mona Lisa," Mike opined.

By now I'd realised what had happened.

"Mister Outer Space?" I enquired.

"Indubitably," Mike replied, "to the tune of fifty!"

I proposed the toast:

"Here's to lunatics!"

We drank with mock solemnity. I looked at the clock.

"We've got to go, Mike," I said, "our public is waiting."

I guided the reluctant Mac to the door.

"Come back after the show," Mike called, "we'll celebrate tonight."

As Mac and I left, he ordered another Scotch.

"Vintage," he added.

Chapter 12

Despite Mac's protests we got as far as Soho Square before he complained to passersby about his loss. From there to the New Theatre he ranted wildly about his 'missed nectar'; waving his stick at everyone.

"Flagons of Rhenish; Gone-all-gone. Bring me a jug of sack, vassal," etc.

I guided him to the 'New'. The queue was a long one with only ten minutes to go before it went in.

"Ladies and Gentlemen, Good Evening," I commenced.

"Good evening, my foot!" Mac shouted, "It's a bloody cold evening and these ladies and gentlemen are a frozen-faced pack of bores, about to be bored for two hours by another pack of bores, in this oversize lavatory calling itself a theatre."

"My colleague," I apologized, "is, of course, quoting," I tried to save the situation, "from George Orwell's *Animal Farm*. To continue…" I went on quickly, "here is an excerpt from Shakespeare's *Hamlet*."

I started solemnly:

"To be or not to be? That is the question."

"That is *not* the question!" Mac roared, "The question is," he yelled, pointing his stick at the queue, "how much longer are you idiots going to put up with the tenth-rate rubbish masquerading as theatre in this country? All you morons want is American musicals, American crooners, sex and violence. The only English plays you patronise are Shakespeare's, you snobs,…and he hasn't written a hit in two hundred years!"

A crowd of gawkers blocked both ends of the alley. My retreat was cut off. I tried again:

"Whether 'tis nobler in the mind to suffer the slings and arrows of outrageous fortune."

Mac pulled off his battered hat and thrust it at the crowd. I continued with the speech.

"Pay up," he barked, "pay up for the greatest skint actors in London." He waved his stick at them menacingly. I got as far as, "Perchance to dream," when I noticed my Luncheon Vulture Gertrude, with a tall heavily-built man, watching me from a step behind the crowd. Damn it, I thought. But I've got to finish this speech now. I got through it somehow, with Mac cursing and swearing as he passed along the queue. Thank heaven the queue started in as I finished with, "Thus conscience does make cowards of us all."

Before Mac had finished the bottling, I turned and walked rapidly across St. Martin's Lane, just avoiding a passing car. I don't remember how I got there, I was too upset to care.

But I reached Covent Garden, visited the toilet, then wandered on to Waterloo Bridge.

Chapter 13

It was quiet standing there, looking down at the river. I had a feeling of timelessness, of insignificance, of futility. I recalled my childhood, the war coming and me joining the forces. My first love affair. My first disillusion. Of going broke to Paris and back. And of the people I had known who had made life a happier experience. I felt the serrated edge of the 2/- in my pocket. I felt hungry. I walked to a fried fish shop I knew off the Strand, and bought some fish and chips wrapped in a newspaper. One of these days, I thought, looking at the printed sheet, I must read a newspaper.

I passed through the Embankment Gardens. Trying not to embarrass the couples rolling on the grass, I looked up at the Shell Mex clock. It was eight-ten and too late for the Empire or any other theatre queue. I took the underground to Tottenham Court Road on the way to The Wheatsheaf. A drink, I felt, would cheer me up. In the railway carriage, I got to thinking about Mike. I couldn't help envying him his windfall.

Alighting at Tottenham Court Road, I crossed Oxford Street. Walking up Rathbone Place I met Gypsy Larry. He wore a cloth cap and chequered jacket as usual, with his scarf held together by the silver top from a Lyons mustard pot.

"'Allo Charlie. How's the acting?"

He blinked under the glare of the street lamp we were under and moved into a doorway. Larry didn't like the light. In fact he only came out at night time. He passed the day sleeping in his shuttered room off the Euston Road. Larry's heyday was in the 30s, when he got up to every fiddle in the book and salted away enough money to keep him independent now. His only expense apart from fifteen-bob rent, was tins of sardines. He ate nothing else, drank only water and collected tobacco from available ashtrays and pavements. Once, he told me, he attempted to vary his diet with a tin of salmon.

"I only 'et 'arf of it," he said reminiscently, "then grabbed the nearest sardine tin."

At the moment he was picking his ear with a matchstick.

"I've got somefing I bin meanin' to bring dahn fer yer."

"Sorry Larry," I said, "my mind was miles away. What's that you say?"

He repeated it, "*The Green Room Book of Theatre Personalia.* Nineteen-o-nine, it was published."

"That's very thoughtful of you Larry," I said, "could you leave it in the Alex with Michael for me?"

"'Avent got a gaff yet eh?" he guessed knowingly. He patted my shoulder, "Don't worry, Charlie boy. Fings'll turn aht right, believe me."

He paused to adjust his mustard pot scarf ring.

"Well I'm orf to the Billiard 'all. See you up there later if you're around."

"Right-o Larry. Don't forget the *Green Room Book.*"

"I won't forget."

We shook hands and went our ways.

I heard the sound of a flute and voices as I pushed open The Wheatsheaf door.

Chapter 14

It was Mike. I should have guessed. He was jigging on the tabletop, flailing his arms like a maniac and blowing fiercely into a short metal flute. It surprised me he didn't fall. The crowd was singing 'Knees-up Mother Brown' and clapping the rhythm in time with Mike's movements. I waited until the song and dance finished, then waved a hand at him from where I stood by the door. He saw me and waved back. A fat man laughing loudly helped him down from the table. He staggered over to me, his eyes shining.

"Charles, you schizophrenic Thespian. That means half-baked actor. Have a big drink on the establishment. That means me. Everyone else is."

"I'm not very happy Mike," I confessed, "Don't want to spoil your fun; but I could do with a pint of bitter."

"Pint of bitter and a whisky chaser for my friend," Mike called, "and as you're feeling low," he produced a bottle of pills, "have a Dexedrine or two and get high."
He swallowed three or four, and when the bitter and whisky arrived, washed them down with the whisky.

"I feel as great as Leonardo da Vinci himself," he said flamboyantly. I felt embarrassed by his high spirits. I refused a pill and started sipping the bitter. The noise of talking was so loud, we had to almost shout in each other's face to be heard.

"Mac was in half an hour ago looking for you. He left this for you," pulling a pound note from his inside pocket, "It's your share of the busking, Mac said." He turned to the crowd and waved the note, "This is what Charley here made tonight for doing Shakespeare in public and running away." They all laughed boisterously.

"Don't play about Mike. I'm not in the mood," I said rather sharply.

Mike pulled his flute from his top pocket and blew a loud note. The talking quietened and Mike pushed some empty glasses off the counter. They tinkled into fragments on the floor. He jumped up and perched on the counter.

"Ladies and Gentlemen," he said imitating my voice, "in the short time you have left before going into a short time." Laughter.

"Mike," I said loudly, "shut up and forget that stuff!"

"In the short time," he continued. More laughter.

"Shut up you stupid clown!" I shouted, "you're nothing but an artist con-man."

He looked dazed and baffled and, I remember, a little hurt. I slammed the beer mug on the counter, flung open the door and strode out.

I had walked as far as the '91' before I noticed a tear trickling down my cheek. That had been our first quarrel. At the '91', I dragged my feet down the steps to the basement and looked vaguely at the faces. The evening's upsets and my lack of sleep were dazing me a bit. The place was almost empty as was usual on Mondays. Just a few drifters, some dozing. Ricky was sitting alone in a corner. I moved to his table. He looked up from his writing and smiled when he saw it was me. That cheered me up a lot.

"Care for a coffee Charles? You look a little shaken."

"Thanks Ricky. I'd like one very much."

He beckoned to George, the cook, and gave the order.

"Who are those five scribbling over there?" I whispered, pointing to a group of scraggy-looking bums, seated across the room. Ricky looked and answered, "Oh that's Bernard Kops, Bill Hopkins and Frank Norman. The thin one in a roll-neck sweater and horn-rimmed specs, sitting alone, is Colin Wilson. I don't think they'll ever amount to anything much."

Ricky changed the subject.

"I looked in at The Wheatsheaf earlier. Mike told me about his "happy event". But the atmosphere was too rowdy for me, so I came on here."
George brought the coffee.

"I suppose, you're going back to Hampstead shortly, Ricky," I said, "Pity 'cause I could do with some company tonight. Even yours," I joked, "It gets lonely enough wandering the streets at night anyway, without feeling "brought down" as well."

"As it happens," Ricky said "I'm 'Doing a Skipper'[7] myself tonight."

"How come?" I asked, surprised.

"Well," he explained, "Millie has gone home to Manchester to get her parents consent for her passport, as she's under twenty-one. If they give it, we are going to Paris tomorrow."
I gasped, "How wonderful for you."

"Not so very wonderful," he broke in, "I'll have to put up with Millie."

"Consider your good fortune," I consoled him, "You'll be getting out of this set-up. Paris is good for poetry. In a few days you'll be writing like Francois Villon."

"Better, I hope," said Ricky, "That's the spirit! Now I'm cheering you up!"

"Of course," I realised sadly, "I shall miss you…very much you know."
We were silent for a long minute. Then I noticed a girl in a neat fur-collared coat, her hair drawn into a small bun on top of her head. She gazed at me hypnotized. It was Geraldine…damn it! I finished my coffee.

---

[7] Sleeping rough. Ed.

"Let's leave this place," Ricky said.

We stood up. He buttoned his coat. As we walked to the door George collected Ricky's bill. Ricky told him he might be going away tomorrow.

"Is this so?" George said, and looked at me disbelieving.

"Yes, George," I said, "Ricky's off on a well-earned holiday."

George shook Ricky's hand saying, "All of the very best," in his Greco-English baritone.

Geraldine clung to my hand as we mounted the stairs to the street. Ricky paused on the landing.

"I think I'll go to the toilet," he said, "Charles, would you care to join me?"

"Wait here," I said to the girl and walked after Ricky into the back yard. The toilet consisted of the wall and the gutter at the foot of it. We urinated.

"Charles, my friend," he said, "I think your red-headed girl is very attractive."

"Thank you," I said, "I don't feel in the mood to find anyone attractive. Would you care to take over?"

I had already sounded the strength on the way up the stairs and benefitted to the tune of 5/-. We rejoined Geraldine in Charlotte Street, only this time Ricky took her other hand. She didn't seem to notice.

"Let's go to the Billiard Hall in Windmill Street," I suggested.

I told him Gypsy Larry had been on his way there.

"I'd rather not, Charles," Ricky said timidly, "the place is full of men. Besides, Gypsy Larry always smells like sardines."

We were crossing Oxford Street now; the traffic was thinning and Ricky was talking quietly to the girl. She seemed to be listening. I thought to myself, I will go up and see Larry and leave these two to enjoy themselves.

Chapter 15

We turned into Dean Street when I heard a crash of breaking glass.

"What's that?" said Ricky and put his am round the girl. We only wondered for a moment. A figure came running towards us from the corner being chased by a tall man, waving something in his hand which glistened in the street light. They came nearer and I saw it was a broken bottle. The taller of the two, a rough-looking character, wearing a jacket much too wide for him, caught up with the one in front, stopping him with a whack across the head with the bottle. He collapsed on his knees, just opposite the doorway in which we stood, not daring to move.

"You bastard!" the tall one snarled, kicking his victim in the ribs, "You dirty copper's nark!"

The shorter man tried to stand, and caught another kick, this time in the groin. He doubled, catching a knee in his face. Moaning, he fell sprawling on his back. Quickly his attacker jumped on him, digging his knee into his victim's stomach. Raising the broken bottle, he brought it down with a curse into the other's face. Blood spurted onto the pavement.

I looked at Ricky, and without a word the three of us ran as fast as we could, all the way along the back turnings, through Brewer Street, into Windmill Street. Out of breath, we were too stunned to speak, till we reached the entrance of the Billiard Hall.

"I'm going up to see Larry and have a much needed cup of tea," I gasped.

Ricky and Geraldine stood panting on the pavement. I remembered who was with me, "Why don't you two go for a walk," I said.

"What time is it?" Geraldine asked suddenly. I looked at the illuminated clock on the corner of Shaftesbury Avenue. She followed my eyes:

"11 o'clock," she gasped, "Mother will wonder whatever has happened to me."

"For Heaven's sake don't tell her!" I said.

"We are staying the weekend at Cumberland Hotel, Marble Arch. I promised to be in by 12 at the latest. Is it far?"

"It's only a five minute walk from here," I lied, "Ricky will take care of you."

I winked aside to him, saying, "Come upstairs for me when you've seen her home."

I left them there.

I climbed the two flights of stairs to the Billiard Hall feeling a little calmer now, though out of breath. At the door the big ex-boxer with the battered face asked me for my membership card.

"Do I look like a copper?" I said, "Anyway I've seen you in the 'Club Room' and in the other place, lots of times."

He looked baffled, but my stubbly chin and long hair reassured him. He attempted a smile and let me in. The atmosphere of tobacco smoke and sweat, all warm and choking, dazed me for a moment, but it was cozy in here and strictly for men only. No women at all, not even 'queers'. The eight billiard tables were all occupied with players, most of them in shirt sleeves and braces. I walked around to the counter. Inside a glass cabinet lay undistinguished buns. Larry was sitting on a bench talking earnestly to four smartly dressed youngish men. He was tearing open some cigarette ends he had doubtless collected. He put the tobacco into the palm of his left hand. The four lads I recognised. They had been busy the past few months making a living selling stolen volumes collected from the book shops in the Charing Cross Road.

"Ullo Charlie," Larry greeted me. He pulled a cigarette paper from his top pocket. I sat down next to him. The four lads didn't say anything. Larry leaned over to me confidentially.

"These boys nearly got lumbered in 'Charlies' today," he said in my ear. 'Charlies', I recollected, was their trade name for Foyles bookshop. The leader of the quartet who had a beaky nose and a growth of fluffy mouse hair on his chin said:

"Yeah, we was leaving the Art Department with two bags full of gear, when three dicks lumbered us in the doorway," he paused to relive the scene, "We had to have a barney. So in the scuffle we lorst our gear. I banged one of them. A cross-eyed geezer he was. I caught him straight across the boat-race with me bag and made a run for it on me toes."

Larry finished rolling his cigarette, licked the paper, put it in his mouth and asked the lad next to him for a light.

"How did you others get away?" I asked.

"We kicked and kneed and nutted," another explained, "Then orf on our toes till we all met up here just now."

A voice at the nearby billiard table caught my attention. I looked over and, in the dim light reflected from its green baize top, a short stocky man stood pointing his cue at the marker, who stood at the score-board beside me.

"I've got five nicker on this game," the cue holder hissed, "and I think you're fiddling the score."

"Don't talk like a mug, Ben," his partner said in a cheery way, "Bill's alright, I've known him for years."

"I'll bet you have," the stocky character replied, "and how much are you bunging for the fiddle?"

The score marker's voice at my elbow exclaimed, "Are you saying I'm lowering your score?"

The short man dropped the cue and picked up a black snooker ball. He closed one eye, lifted the ball, took aim, and bowled it, like he was on a cricket pitch, straight at the score-keeper. The black ball of ivory thudded against the wall just to the right of me. He should have stuck to Billiards. Cauliflower head was yelling from the doorway, trying to be heard above the din.

"Coppers!" he bawled, "The law's comin' up the stairs!" Amid the jostling and noise, I was crowded down the stairs and crammed into a van. It was, I realized, a police van. It started moving. In the van everyone was quiet and we were soon locked away in cells.

Chapter 16

I was celled with two large and ugly villains, whose expensive suits had suffered badly from the billiard hall affray. The third was a thin, white faced runt who sat cross-legged on the floor as soon as the door-key turned in the lock. The two villains sat on the blanket on the only wooden bench. I rested as best I could on the toilet. I was so tired that I preferred even these surroundings to a night out; walking in the cold, dropping in at the odd coffee stall, waiting till I felt tired enough to face the concrete floor place. I must have dozed.

A gruff voice was saying from what seemed a long way off, "Mind if I 'ave a slash mate?"

It was the largest and ugliest of the tearaways. I moved off the seat to oblige him and continued sleeping on the floor. I woke up screaming. Only it wasn't me, but the skinny paleface. He was spread against the door screaming through the peephole in it, "Give me my gear!" he yelled, "I must have a jolt, I'm going crazy. For God's sake, give me my gear!"

The small sized villain on the bench woke up.

"Shut up mate and try and get some kip," his voice had an edge to it. The other villain snored.

"You've gotta get me a fix," the skinny one gurgled plaintively.

"I'll fix you meself, if you don't shut up!" Small-Size shouted.

Just then the keys rattled, the door opened and skinny dived outside. The door closed and we were left in peace. Small-Size rolled up his trouser leg and pulled some crumpled cigarettes and a matchbox from his sock. He offered me a smoke. I took one. He lit them, saying:

"Need a fag after that little lot. Some people ought to be locked up."

I smoked the cigarette, listening to a talk about the mugs and drug addiction. I dropped the fag-end into the toilet and went back to sleep.

The clanking of the keys woke me. The officer called cheerfully: "Wakey, Wakey," and handed in a tray with three mugs of tea and some toast on it. The large dishevelled villain, who had grown a black eye during the night, passed me a mug. His mate offered the tray of toast. I took a slice.

"When do we get out of here, Screw?" he asked the officer.

"The van'll be taking you on to Bow Street when you've finished breakfast," he answered, "but don't hurry, you may get indigestion."

He shut the door behind him and we heard him chuckling at his joke, through the peephole.

We shared the toast and drank the tea and waited for what seemed an hour or longer. My companions chatted about the last time they had 'got done' by the police. I gathered from the phrases 'Turning over a drum' and 'doing bird' for a 'two stretch', that they had been sentenced to two years imprisonment on a charge of housebreaking. Eventually the door rattled and opened again.

We were led along between the two rows of cells, together with the other overnight trade. Three vans waited in the courtyard for us all. We piled in and travelled without a word. At the end of the journey we were led out of the vans and put into cells again, separately this time. After that I was invited to appear in court. The clerk announced in a dry tone:

"Charles Compton Street of no fixed address. Disturbing the peace," and so on. When the dock was offered to me, I went and stood in it.

"Forty shillings," the Magistrate said.

I was led out of the Courtroom and into the waiting room. I was trying to think of someone who could pay the fine, when an officer came up to me, "Your name Compton Street?" I nodded.

"Sign at the desk for your property and you can go. Your fine's been paid."

I signed and collected 1/6d, and my toothbrush. I walked through the door and down the steps to the street.

Chapter 17

A blonde man, looking very smart in a new suit, with Millie holding his hand, met me on the pavement. Then I recognized it was Ricky and realised what had happened.

"Thanks for getting me out," I said, shaking hands with each in turn.

"It's a pleasure to pay forty bob for someone else's fine," Millie said, "makes a change. Usually it's me for soliciting. I always think of it as a sort of 'income tax'," she joked.

Ricky explained what had happened:

"When I got back to the Billiard Hall last night, the doorman told me about the raid. So I went to Rowten House for the night. When I phoned Millie this morning she told me that her passport was O.K. so she came down and we went shopping. We left our luggage parcels at Victoria Station and came here to see that you were alright."

"Don't let's stand *here*," Millie said with a shudder, "Bogey Stations give me the creeps."

"It's nearly time for Millie and me to get our train, Charles. Departs at 12.47."

We walked along Bow Street towards the Underground station in silence. Suddenly Ricky said, "Before I forget Charles, Geraldine gave me this note for you. It was left at The Wheatsheaf last night."

I said, "Thanks," and took it.

Ricky looked like a story-book millionaire in his grey pinstripe suit, brown suede shoes, soft silk collar and striped tie. The only commonplace effect was his middle-class hair-cut. He must have noticed me looking at him, for he said ruefully:

"I feel so inhibited in this outfit. I'm frightened even to sit down lest I disturb the creases."

We crossed the street to the tube. I wished them both '*Bon Voyage*' and shook hands with Ricky. A tear trickled down his cheek. Millie mopped it off with his breast pocket handkerchief, replacing it carefully. They passed through the barrier and out of sight. I stood for a few moments after they had gone, wondering what would happen to them.

Chapter 18

Then I looked at the note in my hand. It read: 'Ring Mr. Scrimpson, Vic 9257, Vulture.'

I entered one of a row of adjacent phone boxes. After charming the telephone operator for a free call, she put me through.

"Old Vic Theatre Office," stated a bright falsetto which could have been male or female.

"I must have the wrong number."

"Whom do you wish to speak to, please?"

I read the name aloud: "Mr. Scrimpson."

"One moment please, I'll put you through."

"Who is that?" a gruff voice demanded.

I was getting annoyed.

"This is Compton Street," I announced meticulously, "I have a message signed 'Vulture'".

"Compton Street?" he repeated, "I've heard that name before somewhere." He grunted, "Ah yes, I recall. You're the young man Miss Skinner suggested I saw perform outside the New Theatre last night. You have an outstanding talent, young man. I can find a place for you in our company."

It took a full moment for that to penetrate. I thought it over, then I said:

"Thanks for the offer Scrim, but I've seen some of your productions and I'd rather not. Also a 'job' would mean keeping a landlord in rent, so I'd be available for rehearsals every morning and performances every evening, at your disposal."

I heard him gasp, "and the expense of Income tax and taxes to contribute to hydrogen bombs and trips to outer space. Also the bore of learning lines; in short, Mr. Scrimpson: thanks for the offer, but I've had time to see life lately and I'd rather stay the way I am."

There was a long pause and then, "But suppose everyone felt like you. Nobody would ever do anything!"

"On the contrary," I said, "Society would collapse, that's all. And people would have to fend for themselves and think for themselves and see the truth about life. I don't think that will happen, though," I chuckled, "most people are happy and comfortable the way they are. Though atomic bombs and Earth's starving millions sometimes make them wonder."

"Yes," he repeated slowly, as though he was talking to a madman, "I see your point."

"Anyway," I said, "Thank Miss Vulture for trying to do me a favour. And thanks again for the offer Mr. Scrimpson. I'll give you a ring again if your theatre management ever decides to do plays about today's problems. Let's face it, we both do Shakespeare because it impresses the mugs."

I hung up. I was surprised at myself. Three months earlier, the chance of a job with the 'Old Vic' would have seemed the most wonderful thing in the world.

I went into the pub next door and had a glass of bitter to celebrate my freedom both from jail and from society.

Chapter 19

Halfway through the bitter I thought of Mike. I felt so sorry about the quarrel that I just had to straighten it out. Full of resolve, I finished the beer and left the pub. I manoeuvred in and out of the fruit trucks and barrows being loaded in Long Acre, and the jeers from the porters, who doubtless felt intimidated by my unconventional appearance. Emerging at the Coventry Street junction of Charing Cross Road, a 24 bus whisked me Camden

Townwards and I was soon whistling the Beethoven signal under Mike's window. He didn't appear, so using the knocker I rapped the signal loudly. Shortly a shuffling came from within. Then a bedraggled woman aged about fifty and dressed in a faded red housecoat, exposed herself in the doorway.

"Whader yer want?" she piped.

"Michelangelo," I replied, "I believe he moved here from Florence."

"I dono abaht that," she said indifferently, "but Mr. Angelo's been taken orf to the 'ospital this morning."

"What!" I almost shouted, "hospital, what for? Where?"

"I dunno abaht that. Saint George's, I fink they said it was."

The door closed. The shuffling faded.

Saint Georges Hospital. Then it was at Hyde Park Corner. Recovering from my amazement I considered the quickest way to get to Hyde Park Corner. In a few minutes I was at Camden Town crossroads and boarding the underground to Hyde Park. I changed lines at Leicester Square, arriving half an hour later in front of the imposing front of St. Georges. Enquiring at the Reception desk, a scrubbed and starched matron asked me patronisingly;

"Are you a relative?"

"His brother," I lied.

She told me to return at visiting time, 6.30, when I could see him for half an hour. I walked slowly down the steps, looking idly at the facing crossroads packed with vehicles rushing in all directions at once. I turned and looked at the large clock fronting the building: 2.30pm. Four long hours before I could see my friend and I could do nothing but wait. Perhaps I would try to sleep somewhere, I thought, Hyde Park lay on my left. I had heard tell of its virtue as a bedroom in summer. Just now it was a little too cold for comfort. St. James' Park stretched in front of me. Though the ducks on the lake seemed to enjoy sleeping there, I didn't think I would. It would have to be the reading room at South Africa House again. I would be awakened at 5.30 when it closed.

I manoeuvred through the traffic at Hyde Park Corner, walked briskly between the avenue of bare trees, beside Buckingham Palace, across the square of waterless fountains, and beside the row of bare trees flanking Pall Mall. Stopping for a moment to watch the Palace Guards who, wearing red coats, furry hats and rifles, either sat like statues on horses or marched to and fro like machines. I hurried on past a group of four foreign-looking men covered with cameras, taking photographs of the scene.

I passed under Admiralty Arch, with its vast inscription, in Latin, I think. Past the memorials—monuments to those Englishmen slain by Indians, Africans, Dutchmen and others. Across Trafalgar Square, past more memorials and through the portals of South Africa House.

Chapter 20

The Reading Room was spacious. Its windows were over twenty feet high. It was walled with laden dusty bookshelves and furnished with a long wooden table covered in magazines. I suppose they were South African magazines. Around the table, and spaced against the bookshelves, were the chairs. Large, high-backed arm chairs, bulging with stuffing. They seemed to me to resemble mattresses folded in the middle.

As usual, I pretended to sort a magazine at the table, and took one with me to a corner armchair away from the door. I sat down slowly, savouring the upholstery, then leaned forward, and untied my shoelaces. I sank back and tried to look interested in the magazine which I propped on my crossed knees. There was a movement from across the room. An elderly tailored gentleman staggered slowly from his chair to the table. Slowly he replaced the magazine and sorted another from the pile. I watched, fascinated by the ritual. He turned and slowly retraced his way back to his chair. He sat again, crossed his knees, and placed the magazine upon them. I looked down and noticed his feet. His shoelaces were undone.

*

"Closing in five minutes, please," a voice called out awakening me. Closing in five minutes; that meant 5.30. That gave me an hour to get to Mike. The magazine, still on my knees, I leaned forward and retied my shoelaces. I stood up and staggered to the table replacing the magazine, as did the other readers. I passed the well-tailored gentleman in the hall doorway and helped him on with his heavy chequered overcoat.

"Thanks for the lift," he drawled, chuckling throatily, "useful place to spend an afternoon."

"Very useful," I agreed, wished him "Cheerio" and left.

I crossed to the square and watched the pigeons. Suddenly I felt hungry. Damn it! The warm puffed after-sleep sensation in my face soon went in the icy air. I dug my hands deeper into the pockets of my overcoat, searching for coins in the lining. Among the coins I felt a crisp piece of paper. I pulled it out. It was a pound note.

It was unbelievable! Then I remembered. It was my share of last night's busking with Thesby. I went straight down Trafalgar Square Underground and bought a shave in the toilet. I came up feeling very fresh and on top of the world. I called to a passing cab. He pulled up.

"Driver," I said, "take me to Buckingham Palace and stop at a fruit barrow on the way."

Chapter 21

He looked at me queerly as I got in. I relaxed on the spongy seat. We cruised smoothly around the square and stopped at a barrow on the corner of the Strand. I got out and bought a bag full of apples and oranges. I climbed back into the cab and we passed under Admiralty Arch reminding me of my earlier frozen journey. The view seemed different somehow. Sort of impersonal. Even the avenue of naked trees looked unreal. I picked an apple from the bag and took a bite. As we approached the fountains in front of the Palace the driver slowed down and slid back the communicating window.

"Er...excuse me Guv'ner, but you did say Buckingham Palace?"

I affected a very posh voice, "What the Dickens is the matter my man?" I took another bite as the cab stopped, "Do you want an apple, is that what it is?"

I offered him the bag. He ignored it.

"Then why hev you stopped? Hev you run out of juice?"

"Er...no, it ain't the juice Guv, but yer didn't mean fer me ter take yer right up to the Palace did yer?"

"Right up to the front gates," I assured him, "I boarded your vehicle having imparted most clear and explicit instructions regarding my intentions. If you keep me waiting any longer, I shall make a tally and deduct this pointless conversation from the extortionate amount displayed on your clock."

He was silent for a minute, then he turned and looked at my scruffy clothes. This decided him. He left his seat, walked round to the side and opened the door. He looked at me as though he thought I was crazy.

"You were quite right Sir," he said attempting a smile, "I *have* run out of juice as you said, so I will have to drop you here."

"This is an outrage of incompetence!" I said descending to the pavement.

"There'll be no charge Sir" he said, and pointing he added, "Buckingham Palace is there, on the other side of that fountain."

"The fountain isn't working," I said, "someone has bungled the water plumbing again."

Before I'd finished speaking he was back in his cab and driving away quickly. I walked across past the fountain. The sentries were still marching up and down like machines in their furry hats twenty sizes too big. I walked once more between the avenue of trees at the side, tossing my third apple core into the gutter as I crossed Hyde Park Corner. The clock on the Hospital read 6.35. I hurled up the steps and introduced myself again to Miss Frozen Face. She regarded my shaven chin from an approving hygenic viewpoint.

"Michelangelo," she informed me with a smirk, "is on the second floor, Ward six, bed no. 8."

She gave me instructions how to get there. I thanked her and followed the directions.

A very pretty nurse escorted me to Mike's bed. I resisted the urge to make a date with her.

"Visitor for you Mr. Angelo," she said.

Chapter 22

Mike was sitting up in bed, staring vacantly. When the nurse spoke, he didn't move, didn't say a thing. I sat in the chair beside the bed. The nurse smiled at me and was gone, I was amazed at Mike's silence.

"Mike it's me; Charles," I said.

Still he didn't move.

"It's too late," was all he said in an empty voice.

"For Heaven's sake tell me what's happened Mike... I went round to your gaff this morning and some woman told me you were here. I came at once but had to wait for hours before they would let me see you."

Mike turned and looked at me.

"And I've brought you some fruit."

I showed him the bag. He put his hand on mine.

"Thanks very much for coming," he said quietly, "I've been feeling so hopeless and alone."

He took an apple from the bag and looked at it.

"Charles, it's incredible, but I'll tell you what's happened."

He put the apple down and gazed at the foot of the bed. Then he said:

"Last night, after you left The Wheatsheaf, I kept on drinking and chewing Dexedrine pills till closing time. When I left I was roaring drunk and high as a kite. As I got to the White Tower Restaurant in Charlotte Street I saw a wealthy looking group standing outside it, apparently waiting for a taxi. So I did the old trick of staggering and collapsing on the ground in front of them. When they bent over me to see what had happened, I started the routine of clutching at my stomach and moaning, "My guts, my guts, I haven't eaten for a fortnight." Suddenly a real pain shot through me, right in my stomach. It must have been all that Dexedrine and beer. The pain got unbearable and I screamed out in agony. My audience took a step backwards, then the taxi arrived and the driver came over to see what was going on. I was in real agony, yelling and rolling all over the pavement. They asked me who I was, and where I lived. "I've been poisoned," I yelled, "They've poisoned me!" I don't remember clearly what happened then. I was helped into the taxi and must have fainted. When I came to myself I was lying on my back with white-coated figures peering down at me. For a moment I wondered if there was truth in that Heaven business, and that perhaps I was there. The pain in my guts was gone. I saw these figures had instruments in their hands and suddenly I felt terrified. I realised I was helpless, in strange hands, in another world. I tried to move, but I didn't have the strength. "He's awake now," one white coated figure said and moved towards me, "Your name and address," he demanded. I was petrified. "Let me go!" I screamed, "Let me out of here!" "It's all right," he said, "we are taking care of you." "I don't want you bastards to take care of me! Let me out!" I screamed, "leave me alone!" I exhausted myself quickly in my weakened state and lay back gasping. The figure continued as if nothing had happened, "When you came in last night you were in such a bad state yelling and raving about your stomach, that we diagnosed an ulcer and operated. Afterwards we realised you hadn't anything more than acute indigestion." I was now petrified at the cool way they talked, as if I was a fugitive from the butchers. Then they started another line of patter, "You had no identification when you were brought in. Will you tell us your name, address and next of kin, please?" I liked the "kin" bit. These monsters had me at their mercy. "Michael Angelo," I replied. "Come now, that's not your real name, is it?" "Yes it is!" "You can do better than that. How about your address and next of kin?" "I don't happen to have an address." "You're just trying to be difficult, aren't you now?" "No, I am not. My name's Michael Angelo, I've no bloody address, I don't want no bloody address, least of all here. And my next of kin are all those who are trying to carry on living in a world full of licensed murderers like you and all the rest of your so-called civilization!" I was exhausted again and they conferred among themselves in the corner away from me. I heard odd words. "Unbalanced. Anti-Social. Irrational. Confinement. Rehabilitation. Maladjusted." Slowly they moved around me, into the circle of light from above my head like silhouettes at the sacrificial altar. I was petrified into silence. "We have decided to send you to an institution. For your own good." "What sort?" I demanded. "An institution for mental—ah—readjustment." "You can't do it!" I screamed, "Let me get up. Let me go. I'm a human being. Let me out of here!" I felt hands on my arm and the prick of a needle. I woke up here about an hour ago. I haven't dared open my mouth."

"Mike," I said, trying to reassure both him and me, "that all sounds like a dream. A nightmare. Look, I'll call that pretty nurse over. Now you're yourself again, you'll be out of here in a twinkling. Nurse…oh nurse," I called. She came over, "My friend—er, brother—is all right now, isn't he? I mean he'll be leaving today, I suppose, eh?"
She looked at me for a minute.

"Can I speak to you for moment?" she said. I went over. "I am afraid Mr. Angelo will not be leaving," she confided quietly, "You see he was certified this morning and will be transferred to a mental institution shortly."
I thanked her dully and turned back to Mike. He read the message in my eyes. I sat beside him for what seemed an eternity.

"I'll look after your things, back at the gaff, till you come…," I broke off, lost for what to say.

He put a limp hand on my arm.

"Look after my paintings for me. And Charles! Come
and see me tomorrow and bring a sketching block and some
pencils."

"Course I will," I got up abruptly and left as if in a dream.

Chapter 23

Wandering out into the dark street, noisy with racing traffic
jostling the crowds of frozen-faced people, I found my way
along Park Lane to Marble Arch. Orators full of self-importance
were yelling at their audiences of hypnotised admirers. As
always the favourite was the cry, "Be saved. Repent you
miserable sinners!" from one; "The workers aren't as well off as
the employers!" from another; "There is prejudice against the
foreigner in this country!" from yet another. 'Yes,' I thought to
myself, 'Repent and be saved indeed! After two thousand years
it's time people got wise to that old baloney. And as for the
workers: they all dreamed of the day when they too could
demand a limousine and a fortune in the bank, getting it out of
someone else's sweated labour. And when it comes to prejudice,
there is also prejudice against the natives of a country from the
foreigners, and even their own countrymen, as I knew only too
well.'

I wandered along Oxford Street looking at the goods
temptingly displayed in the brilliantly lighted windows of the
buildings hundreds of feet high. The fine clothes, jewellery, cars,
washing machines, radios, television sets, cookers. In fact, the
hundred-and-one articles that men spent their lives to acquire.
And suddenly it struck me in a flash of awareness. That it was
all a sham, a façade, a huge confidence-trick that made men
slaves. I knew then the answer to that eternal question I had so
long been asking myself: 'Why do you live?' The word was *live*.

Because we live by fulfilling ourselves with the dignity of being human and sufficient unto ourselves.

At the comer of Rathbone Place, Palma was croaking an aria of Puccini to the disinterested passersby. He saw me and stopped.

"Compton Street," he said, "why do you call yourself Compton Street? It's an address not a name."

"Exactly, Palma," I replied.

And as I looked over his shoulder at the lamps in Soho Square, they glowed like little candles in the fog.